Julia Marlowe's Story

BOOKS BY E. H. SOTHERN

THE MELANCHOLY TALE OF ME: MY REMEMBRANCES
MATTER FOR A MAY MORNING

Julia Marlowe's Story

by E. H. Sothern

EDITED BY FAIRFAX DOWNEY

RINEHART & COMPANY, INC.

NEW YORK   TORONTO

Published simultaneously in Canada by
Clarke, Irwin & Company, Ltd., Toronto

Library of Congress Catalog Card Number: 53–10923

Dedication

To Charles Edward Russell

My dear Charles:

I dedicate this record of my hopes and fears and accomplishment—such as it be—to you. For your early sympathy with my purpose, your understanding and generous support sustained me in the dark days of trial and comforted me during the years when I waited, with some wonder at the obduracy of the gods, for my girlhood's dreams to come true. I look back on your long friendship as one source of my strength—on the timely word which supported my courage and helped me to maintain the principles in which I believe, to fortify my faith in the frail issue and to uphold my determination that I must not surrender.

My story as here set down, while it may supplement your own generous and kindly tribute, *Julia Marlowe: Her Life and Art,* necessarily approaches the adventure from a different and more intimate point of view. While you, mostly separated by time and space from my labor, encouraged me as an onlooker, this personal narrative concerns itself with those more immediately associated in my work and some with whom I came more constantly in contact.

But your watchful care and regard for my fortunes have per-

v

haps been a more potent influence than that of any one person I have known. Now that my career is over, and I have been able, on the brink of retirement, to contemplate in peace and security the turmoil of many years of incessant activity in a calling I have loved, I greet with affection and thankfulness one to whom I owe a debt. Your appreciation and solace at those times when a friend was in need proved you a friend indeed. My gratitude to you always.

JULIA MARLOWE SOTHERN

Author's Foreword

"Think of a fact—double it—add some fiction to it—multiply the sum by surmise, add a sufficient amount of quotation! Divide the result into chapters—take away the fact you first thought of, and a biography remains."

Thus a caustic commentator described the modern tendency in recording the lives of great men. One would think that such a process was due merely to the poverty of material. In the present instance, facts are as plentiful as blackberries—the difficulty has been only one of selection—for the subject of these memoirs has been busy with conflicts and fruitful in opinions.

The story of Julia Marlowe is so much a part of the American Theatre that I have often pleaded she should relate it herself. This she has been disinclined to do, so I have ventured to tell the tale of her unique adventure as she has so often repeated it to me. To lend vitality to the narrative, I have made her speak in the first person, in the hope that, to quote the clown in *The Winter's Tale* it may prove "a doleful matter merrily set down" or at least "a very pleasant thing indeed and sung lamentably."

E.H.S.

Editor's Foreword

The autobiography of a great actress, written by her husband and co-star as she told it to him, has proved a fascinating story to one given the pleasant task of editing it. It would seem so, I believe, without my still vivid memories of Julia Marlowe playing Juliet and Rosalind and Viola—a lovely girl with whom a young fellow could fall in love even though she was acting Shakespeare, dramas that had seemed rather dull in college classrooms but never were again after she made them live.

This book will, I think, also hold the interests of readers who never saw Julia Marlowe on the stage. For it has the perennial appeal of a success story, the story of a girl who spared no effort to reach her goal. Here, too, is the glamor of the theatre, embodied by one who cast its spell upon many thousands for most of four decades. Here are life and color and lively comedy, offstage and on. Not least, this is the narration of a career of public service: the true entertainment Julia Marlowe so widely gave, performances praised by critics, played to full houses and rewarded by honors and wealth.

In the background of this volume stand other books with an important bearing on its making. Before setting down Julia Marlowe's story, E. H. Sothern, whose taste for writing was second only to his fondness for the theatre, had brought out his own autobiography, *The Melancholy Tale of Me* (New York. Scribner. 1916). Next appeared Charles Edward Russell's *Julia Marlowe: Her Life and Art* (New York. Appleton.

1926), a competent, commendable biography in the scholarly tradition. That work, greatly admired and appreciated both by Miss Marlowe and Mr. Sothern as testified to by her dedication of this book to Mr. Russell, might have precluded anything further on the same subject from Mr. Sothern's pen. However, the long association of the two stars on the stage and their devoted life as husband and wife determined otherwise.

Consequently Mr. Sothern wrote the present book which, in Miss Marlowe's words to her earlier biographer, "necessarily approaches the adventure from a different and more intimate point of view." Because it does so indeed and contains much material not in the Russell work, publication seemed amply justified. Yet Mr. Sothern's account of his wife's career was still in manuscript at his death in 1933, and though it was Miss Marlowe's desire that it be published, it had not been put into print when she died in 1950. Her wishes, as expressed in her will, are hereby carried out.

In editing the manuscript, I have excised passages with no bearing on Julia Marlowe's story and have omitted addenda containing her views on a municipal theatre since they are concisely stated in Chapter 17. For the general reader I have identified persons whom Mr. Sothern only names. Where it seemed needful, I have supplied background of the times. I have added a chapter covering the latter years of Miss Marlowe's life and the tributes rendered when she died. Title, chapter headings and notes are mine.

Fairfax Downey

New York City, 1953

Contents

List of Illustrations

Julia Marlowe's Story

chapter 1

"What Are You Going To Be?"

It was my fortune to perceive as a child what was necessary for success and to be gifted with that determination which enabled me to overcome many obstacles apparently unsurmountable.

I, Julia Marlowe, christened Sarah Frances Frost, was born August 17, 1865, in an environment which gave me neither educational nor social advantages. My birthplace was the village of Caldbeck in Cumberland, England—Cumberland, the Lake District, beloved of Keats, Shelley, Tennyson, Browning, Wordsworth, Coleridge, Southey. Caldbeck was a village of some three hundred inhabitants. My father's name was John Frost. Previous to her marriage my mother had been Sarah Hodgson. My father's father had kept an inn in the small town of Maryport and later one in Carlisle called "The Red Lion." My father in his boyhood had, as all the country people did, to learn a trade. He was apprenticed to a bootmaker for seven years and became in a small way famous as the most expert workman at his bench in all the countryside.

I recall my father as a large, brown-haired, very handsome man with dancing blue eyes, a general favorite. He was devoted to the sporting and athletic diversions which engross all classes, high and low, in England. He kept horses and not only rode in the country races but drove a drag with a four-horse team to and from the course. He wrestled, he boxed, he gloried

3

in cockfighting. His greyhounds were the swiftest in all the country roundabout. He was ever gay and debonair, a great playmate for his children, with his rollicking songs: *Ride a Cock-horse, The Rocky Road to Dublin, Do Ye Ken John Peel?*

My mother was of a more sober disposition. She belonged to the Wesleyan faith and governed her household with a wise frugality. All our family spoke the Cumberland dialect; my mother kept it throughout her life.

Our family consisted of four daughters and one son. My parents ran a small shop, one end of which was what may be called a general store. At the other end my father practiced his trade. I went to school when I was three, not so much to acquire knowledge as to be out of my mother's way; but I learned nothing. My time was spent sitting before the fire in a low chair cutting out paper dolls. At such a tender age some minds may be open to learning; mine it would seem was not. But back and forth to school I went in the rainy winter weather, and on summer days played on the village green. I remember laboring at my catechism and failing to win a prize offered for the most perfect recitation. I fear I was more than ordinarily backward for my years.

My people, like their neighbors, were chiefly concerned with those activities which would earn their daily bread, and were in no way associated with the theatre or with literature or art. My mother, however, was a great reader of the Bible, with which we early became familiar, and she would frequently recite to us the poems of Robert Burns, many of which she knew by heart.

Our house in the village of Caldbeck was small, built of stone with a slate roof. There was a large garden at the back, truly an English garden, filled with flowers on summer days. The cold brook which gave the village its name ran at the bottom of the garden. The murmuring beehives, the babbling water, the fragrant blossoms—they live still in my memory.

My mother's mother lived at a farm called "Knocker House," high on a hill. Once, when I was there on a visit of some weeks, I was playing on the kitchen floor with my mother's youngest sister, my Aunt Fanny, a child of my own age. My grandmother's kitchen was straight out of Shakespeare's time, just such a one as I later saw in Anne Hathaway's cottage. A great fireplace with deep inglenook and dark corners and recesses for bread, huge fire dogs, a great stone chimney whence one could peer upwards to the sky, beams from which hung sides of bacon, strings of onions and dried herbs for the making of many homely remedies; shining brass, pewter, crockery; a handmade carpet; a long window with small panes. This kitchen was the common sitting room of the cottage.

My Aunt Fanny and I were discussing the inhabitants of Noah's Ark, and an argument arose. My playmate must have spoken sharply, for my grandmother said to her reprovingly, "You must speak kindly to your niece, little Frances. She is going a long way off. You may never see her again."

That was the first intimation I had had of my mother's proposed journey to America, following my father,* who had pre-

---

* C. E. Russell's biography of Julia Marlowe states that her father, John Frost, fled to America as the result of an accident. Driving his drag in an impromptu race with a neighbor, Frost, passing his rival, flaunted his whip in triumph. The lash flicked the other man who screamed that his eye had been knocked out. It was only a crude joke—no injury had been done—but Frost left England in panic, never learning the truth until some time later. In the United States, still fearful of prosecution, he changed his name and that of his family to his mother's maiden name of Brough. Thus his daughter, Sarah

ceded her by some months. It had been his ambition to seek his fortune in the United States, and he had now sent for his family.

During the weeks I had been at "Knocker House," my mother had sold her home and live stock. Proceeds added to her small capital, saved with much care and sacrifice, amounted to about three thousand pounds, sterling. She sewed the bank notes in her clothing and, gathering her brood of children about her, ventured forth. My grandmother, a serious-faced woman with waving brown hair, quite a "magiful" person, packed parcels of tea, eggs, bread, bacon to sustain us on our voyage, and accompanied mother and her five children to Penrith whence we took train for Liverpool to sail on the steamer *Java* for New York.

Never shall I forget the dreadful storm in which our ship was nearly lost. Mother lay crying in her berth, with three of her children clinging to her and a fourth, my small brother three years old, floundering in the inrushing water which flooded the cabin. At last we landed at Castle Garden, New York, where posted placards advised, "Go West, young man." My father, on meeting us, informed us, we were to do just that, and we boarded a train for the long journey.

We found ourselves in Kansas at the end of that year of 1870, a land of prairies and cyclones and Indians. My father had bought a considerable tract of land in Lexington between Kansas City and Olathe. There he had commenced to farm as he had once done in England. The place was stocked with horses, cows and all the necessary farming implements. Also he

---

Frances Frost, became Fanny Brough and was so known through her early stage career. She did not adopt the name "Julia Marlowe" until 1887.

had established a general store to distribute to all the country-side everything from needles to ploughs; in addition he carried on his trade of bootmaking. Mother with her customary energy at once turned part of the dwelling into a millinery store. She was an expert needlewoman and could make all sorts of dainty things and clothes of every description. My father's hopes were high. He believed he had made a great investment in a locality which, with its close proximity to the railway station, might become the site of a new city. Alas, to this day, I believe, our house is the only one in the locality.

How the wind from the prairies howled about our home! Snow piled up in drifts several feet high, almost isolating us from the rest of the world. Trains stalled, and railroad employees came to be warmed at our fire and fed.

Even in the summer time we children—I was then six—dared not venture far from the house, for we were warned that if we were disobedient and wandered away, Indians who prowled around the place would steal us. Yet my mother would fearlessly drive a wagon over the lonely plains to help and comfort another English family also seeking its fortune in Kansas and meeting with no more success than we. Bitter cold and broiling sun, drought or drenching rains oppressed us, transplanted from a gentler climate. One sad winter's day we buried mother's newborn baby in the bleak prairie.

Conquered at last, we moved back East to Ohio. We lived successively in Ironton, Portsmouth, and later in Cincinnati where my father practiced his trade of bootmaker and I attended the public schools.

In going to and from school in Cincinnati, I stared fascinated at the playbills of the old National Theatre: Madame Morlacchi in *The French Spy*, James Hearne in *Hearts of Oak*. Within me stirred a hot desire to ride horses, to shoot apples off other people's heads, to be a glamorous heroine. Meanwhile my ability to learn had improved with age, for at eleven I achieved the sixth grade. Recitations—poems and dialogues— were my favorites; although I was rarely ever better than second in my other classes, in recitations I was always first.

My first play! It was an epoch in my life, of course, but it was a rare adventure, too. My small brother and I for some mis-conduct had been condemned to the coal cellar and its door was locked. While my brother employed himself investigating rat holes, I sat forlorn at the top of the cellar steps. My back to the kitchen door, I was plunged into sombre thought on the wickedness of grownups who had such awful power over poor, helpless, little girls. Meanwhile my brother climbed on top of the heap of coal and, using the shovel, pushed up the lid of the coal hole which opened on to the pavement. I ran to his assistance. As much inflamed by a sense of injury as I, he pro-posed that we escape into the outside world. He helped me up first and then, by the aid of acrobatics, emerged himself.

Now we were free, my brother suggested that we go to the theatre. Through dealings in bottles, rags and old paper he had the price of admission, so off we dashed hand in hand to see Madame Morlacchi in *The French Spy*. Breathless we reached the theatre and bought two gallery seats for ten cents each.

On the way to the abode of the gods, we saw our faces in a looking glass, faces black with coal dust, piebald, like chimney sweeps, but ablutions were impossible and unnecessary. A dry rub, and we were in heaven.

What a glorious night! The heroine was a female version of Mazeppa, bound to a white horse which rushed through mountain passes. Oh, that I were she! The perilous ride! The golden hair! The limelight! The thunders of applause! When the curtain fell, my brother and I ran home, lifted the lid of the coal hole, dropped back into the cellar and, finding the door now unlocked stole up to bed. Many another time we proceeded by our subterranean route to the plays, and only when trade in old bottles was poor did we miss our one marvelous night a week at the theatre.

Except for those wonderful evenings, I had few pleasures, few playmates. Our home had become a solemn one * of strict discipline. We children were taught that our greatest concern was, "What are you going to be when you grow up?" and "Where will you go when you die?" We were constantly told that shortly we would have to take care of ourselves, that our educational opportunities would be limited. But the daily question was, "What are you going to be?"

For me these days were a time of fruitless yearning. I never knelt down to say my prayers that I did not pray for books, for opportunities—that I did not long for beauty and romance. I have read lately that some practical people wish to eliminate fairy tales from children's reading. Ah, never do that, whoever you may be, but let a child's fancy roam at will through wonderland. I was a child whose dark days and nights were gilded by visions, whose drab life was filled with colors of the rainbow and whispers from the stars.

* John and Sarah Hodgson Frost (Brough) had been divorced and the latter remarried. A hearty dislike developed between the children and their stepfather, a man named Hess, who constantly insisted that the children learn a trade to be able to support themselves.

My heart was set on being able to answer my mother's daily question, "What are you going to be?"

My brother had been told, as I suppose most American boys are, that he could be President of the United States, though being English born that was not possible. Mother was continually citing examples of great personages whom we might grow up to resemble. Once she puzzled me greatly by saying that if I did not give my attention to what I was doing, I should never grow up to be like the Duke of Wellington. She must have meant that I would not equal the Duke's renowned powers of concentration. My mother found it difficult to explain just how we should set about emulating the careers of distinguished persons she held up as examples.

Then one day, as if in answer to my prayers, a book agent came to our house in Cincinnati. His wares consisted of a family Bible, copiously illustrated, and a large volume of Shakespeare with engravings of many celebrated actors and actresses in their best-known roles.

My mother bought the Bible. But I had opened the Shakespeare and seen the portraits of Fanny Kemble as Isabella in *Measure for Measure*, Edwin Forrest in the character of *Richard III*, and Barry Sullivan as *Hamlet*, with the Ghost in the background. Imploringly, fervently, I promised my mother I would wash more dishes and make more beds and help harder with all the housework if only I could have that book of Shakespeare. We compromised the matter on my mother's offer, "We'll let your twenty-five cents a week allowance be the weekly installment paid on the book." To that I joyfully agreed, sacrificing my weekly purchases of lollipops. And so I came by my first Shakespeare.

Most people say the Bible and Shakespeare—but I confess that from my earliest remembrance, after I owned that prized book, for me it was Shakespeare and the Bible.

The saddest parts of plays impressed me most. Light and airy comedies, which I found such a joy in later life, at that time I passed by with scant notice. In the Shakespeare I marked particular speeches which appealed to me, for instance Hamlet's lines:

> Be thou as chaste as ice, as pure as snow,
> Thou shalt not escape calumny.

In that I suppose I was not unlike most children who find a wretched joy in being delightfully miserable. Of course I had underlined

> She pined in thought
> And with a green and yellow melancholy
> She sat like patience on a monument,
> Smiling at grief.

and

> Oh, break my heart, poor bankrupt,
> Break at once.

and

> He was not born to shame.
> Upon his brow shame is ashamed to sit.

Whenever I had a moment free from school hours and my household tasks, I read the plays, the garret my reading room and refuge. While I made beds and shook out the pillows, I declaimed the beautiful poetry even as Shakespeare himself is said to have done as he slaughtered calves and sheep for his father's butcher shop.

It was not the singing lines of the Bard I was destined first to utter behind footlights but the witty rhymes and songs of Gilbert and Sullivan.

In a newspaper advertisement I read that children were desired for a juvenile *Pinafore*, and all a-thrill I could scarcely wait to investigate this heaven-sent opportunity. Running an errand for my mother gave me my chance to inquire at the address given, a pawnbroker's shop, owned by one Mr. I. Cohen, who had four daughters in the company, some of them cast for leading parts.

Home I rushed with my news to beg permission from my mother whose consent was necessary before I could be accepted. After considerable hesitation she accompanied me to the Grand Opera House where we met other child recruits for the operetta. My mother was asked a few questions, and after only a brief conversation I was engaged. On the way home I was full of talk about my preparations. With no trunks allowed, my wardrobe was to go into a large leather suitcase, while a bandbox contained my extra bonnet. So I was started on my theatrical career. It was as swift and sudden as that.

I was to leave next morning, and most of the night was spent collecting my few belongings. Next day I was put in the care of a pleasant woman whose daughter also was to be a member of the cast, and away we three started for Vincennes, Indiana, where we found the rest of the Juvenile Opera Company assembled in a small hotel. I then discovered to my surprise that several of the "children" were midgets of mature age. Dick Deadeye was a patriarch of about thirty, Little Buttercup was no chicken, the Captain was past the flush of youth, and some of the ladies had left their dancing days behind them, yet they were smaller than I. They were people from Lilliput.

I was told that my role was to be that of a common sailor, and that my costume would be given to me at the theatre. When I arrived there, I did not even have a rehearsal. I was simply to go on with a dozen other sailor-children and watch what they did.

The wardrobe woman presented me with my costume: a little pair of woolen trousers and a white linen blouse with blue collar. On my head was placed a cap bound with a ribbon emblazoned in gold letters "*H.M.S. Pinafore*," and on my feet black leather, ankle-high slippers. Then the wardrobe mistress dabbed a bit of red on my cheeks and said, "There, that'll do for *you*."

I regarded myself in the glass without enthusiasm, but my spirits were restored on seeing a dozen other small-fry sailors who looked exactly as I did. I heard "First Act" called, and I was told to follow the others, which I did, wondering what would happen next. In a moment I was on stage, hitching my trousers, pulling imaginary ropes, dancing a hornpipe and pretending to sing with the others:

> We sail the ocean blue.
> Our saucy ship's a beauty.
> We're sober men and true
> And attentive to our duty.

I had made my first appearance on any stage.

After a few weeks when I knew all the music, the boy who played Admiral Sir Joseph Porter met with some misfortune and had to go home. I was promoted from the forecastle to the quarterdeck.

Now, at thirteen, I had determined "what I was going to be." For me the theatre was the fairyland of romance for which I had longed, and I was convinced that my career had been launched. How little I realized what toil lay before me!

One day I saw in the lobby of a theatre we were playing in a large photograph of Adelaide Neilson in the role of Imogen in *Cymbeline*, one of my Shakespeare heroines. The portrait was draped in mourning, and I was told that Miss Neilson had been a great actress. At that moment there came into my mind ambition to follow her particular branch of the art of the theatre. I gazed long at this picture, and promised myself I would one day act Imogen.

Touring small towns of the West, we beheld glaring playbills of other troupes: *Ten Nights in a Bar Room* and *Uncle Tom's Cabin*. I grew discontented with the deck of a ship as our only scene of action and with the same lines to be repeated every night. Longing to play other characters, I envied Eliza crossing the ice, pursued by ferocious bloodhounds, a babe in her arms, Uncle Tom in pathetic attitudes, little Eva on her deathbed singing:

> Uncle Tom, oh, set him free.
> Papa, promise this to me.

Vividly I fancied myself as Uncle Tom and soon, having bought an acting version for fifteen cents, I persuaded some of the other children to join me in rehearsing *Uncle Tom's Cabin*, with me of course in the chief part. I must be Uncle Tom! On that point all had to agree.

Rehearsals began when the *Pinafore* company was playing at a small town hall in Michigan. As Uncle Tom, I covered my face with burnt cork and altered my costume from sailor's to slave's. Acting our parts to the hilt, we marched from triumph to triumph. When we reached the end of the play, I felt our glory would not be complete unless the curtain should descend. But how to get the curtain down? There was no stagehand about to lower it.

It was up to me. Though as Uncle Tom I had just died, I jumped from my deathbed and climbed the iron ladder attached to the wall. While the others were delivering final lines with pathos, I unfastened ropes and began to turn the handle of the machine which lowered the curtain.

The final tableau of the play is thus described in the playbook: "Uncle Tom has just given up the ghost, saying with his last breath, 'Heaven has come. I've gotten the victory.' Lighting produces gorgeous clouds tinted with sunlight. Eva, robed in white, is discovered on the back of a milk-white dove with expanded wings as if soaring upward. Her hands are extended in benediction over St. Clare and Uncle Tom who are kneeling and gazing up to her. Impressive music. Slow curtain."

High in the air, I furnished the "slow music," humming loudly and impressively as I released the curtain. Little Eva meanwhile had descended from her snow-white dove (a chair) and had gone down to the first entrance where she was busy taking numerous calls and kissing her hands to an imaginary audience. Down came the curtain, as my impressive music rose triumphant, and banged Little Eva on her little head. She screamed and burst into tears. The cast rushed to her assistance, all shrieking loudly in sympathy and denouncing Uncle Tom, who in panic was descending the ladder.

"Now see what you've done!" they cried. "You'll catch it!"

Uncle Tom rushed to Little Eva and kissed her until her tears mingled on her face with his burnt cork, and the pair resembled chimney sweeps.

Indignant grownups appeared, and there was much scolding and much unreasonable talk after the grown-up fashion. As if people dropped curtains on people's heads on purpose!

We child troupers reminded ourselves more of asylum orphans than strolling players when we were taken out for exercise. We walked two and two, dressed in uniform—small tweed ulsters and caps. We played mostly small towns, one-night stands, which meant traveling on the trains every day. All through the tour I still read my Shakespeare. My only other diversion was playing with a collection of small china dolls, small enough to cram a hundred into a cigar box. With them I satisfied my desire for strange costumes, dressing them fantastically and making up all sorts of stories about them.

Although the tour lasted nine months, I was sturdy and strong and did not suffer any harm from my experiences. The Juvenile Opera adventure was merely a novelty. Public interest waned after a time, the company dissolved, and I returned home.

Having trod the boards, I was sure the theatre was my calling. Next season I was back, as eager as ever. I walked on as a page to Laurence Barrett in *Francesca da Rimini*. I was one of the children in the play *Bob*, performed by Lotta, and a supernumerary in that thrilling drama, *Michael Strogoff, Courier of the Czar.*

But the theatre was now regarded by my mother as too precarious a means of livelihood. My salary in the *Pinafore* company had been seven dollars a week plus my board, which hardly seemed the path to wealth and independence. Mother's former religious prejudices against the theatre revived. Yet though she discouraged my bent, she did not guide me in any other direction.

Mother during those days kept a small hotel and, though quite prosperous, practiced rigid economy. Her children were well cared for, but her constant concern as to our future kept her demanding of us, "What are you going to be?" Well, what could I be? It must be something where I could earn money. First I tried to learn "chart" dressmaking. Next I was led by children who had been my friends in the *Pinafore* company to essay packing gingersnaps in a large bakery. They had become expert, they told me, and made large sums of money at "piece work." All one day I clumsily packed crackers at seventy-five cents a box, but by night I was so ill from the smell of gingersnaps, I could stand no more. My next effort was to become a telegraph operator; after sticking to it several months, I decided that was not my field.

Toward the end of 1881 I found another opportunity in the theatre. I appeared as the boy Heinrich in *Rip Van Winkle* with Robert McWade, playing mostly only in the small towns, once more at a salary of seven dollars a week with board. However, my experience began to embrace a wider horizon, for I was given understudy parts. Once on a half-hour's notice, I was

assigned to play the part of the leading lady who had fallen ill—
I, who was only sixteen years old. I only remember I spoke the
lines after a fashion. My experience with this company was
short lived, since it expired from lack of patronage. With my
seven dollars a week much in arrears, I went back once more to
my mother.

Dejected and discouraged, I began to think that if I were
going to be anything, it certainly was not an actress. I had then
no inkling that my career had really commenced when I
boarded *H.M.S. Pinafore*. In charge of the children's company
for a time had been Miss Ada Dow, an accomplished actress
and student of the art of the theatre. I now became her protégée and apprentice. With Ada Dow as skipper, my ship gave
promise of coming in and someday making port.

chapter 2

Aid from Aunt Ada

Ada Dow—Aunt Ada I soon came to call her—spoke the open-sesame which magically flung wide the portals of the theatre for me. No longer need I ascend to the abode of the gallery gods which my brother and I had reached via the coal hole from the depths of our cellar. For Aunt Ada was a sister-in-law of Robert E. J. Miles, manager of the Cincinnati Grand Opera House, and through her I was privileged to sit in state in the eminence of the manager's box.

New plays, all the galaxy of stars that came to shine in Cincinnati—I never missed a one. I saw Mary Anderson in *Romeo and Juliet*, Laurence Barrett in *The Lady of Lyons* and *Francesca da Rimini*, John McCullough in *Virginius* and *Ingomar*, Maggie Mitchell in the *Pearl of Savoy* and *Fanchon*. I saw tragedy and burlesque. I found good in everything.

Mr. Miles became manager of an ambitious amateur, Miss Josephine Reilly, who was to perform in a repertoire of standard plays: *Pygmalion and Galatea, Romeo and Juliet, Twelfth Night* and *The Hunchback*. Here, thanks to Aunt Ada again, dawned my opportunity. With her as my sponsor, I left the manager's box for backstage and became a member of the company. The part of Master Stephen in *The Hunchback* was made over for me to that of a young boy. Juliet, of course, was the star's prerogative; I played Balthazar. I had to provide my own costumes and I was to receive twenty-five dollars a week

19

and board. With my mother's help and the family dressmaker's, we managed to make costumes, admittedly becoming.

Before the season opened I strenuously studied my parts, devoting a whole month to constant practice of laughter. I was rather a melancholy child and not inclined to boisterous expression, but I realized the necessity for laughter, infectious and gay, in the character of Maria. While doing housework, I laughed in every key, in every mood—sly laughter, scornful, triumphant, mischievous, glad. And when finally I played Maria, my laughter attracted the attention of amiable critics, who acclaimed it contagious, irresistible and natural, though it was purely a product of industry and art.

Aunt Ada was a leading spirit of the company, and through her help I was steadily advanced. The season had scarcely begun before I was understudying all Miss Reilly's parts. It was not half over when I had them letter perfect and had developed decided ideas as to how they should be played. Aunt Ada, moved by my eagerness and zeal, encouraged me continually.

The name with which I was christened, Sarah Frances Frost, does not appear on any playbills of the period. It was Fancy Brough,* as I was then called (Fanny having been transformed into Fancy by the manager's daughter), who was programmed as playing minor roles and understudying the leading lady.

When the season ended, I went with Aunt Ada to the country, to the home of her brother-in-law outside of Cincinnati,

---

* Russell gives a description of Julia Marlowe-to-be at this time, 1883. "She was now eighteen years old, of medium height, slender and frail of aspect, with a pale and rather sallow face, great, dark, and wistful eyes, a head that seemed too big for her body, beautiful, dark-brown hair in bushy ringlets, and a manner off the stage singularly shy and diffident. The odd thing was that on the stage she was all at her ease, sure of herself, with some showing of native grace and intelligence."

where I continued my study of the various characters of Miss Reilly's repertoire. Then with my mother's consent, I became Aunt Ada's pupil and was placed under her protection and care.

Now I took the great step which must ever be memorable to any young actress. Chaperoned by my teacher, I went to New York, Mecca of all things theatrical. I was just eighteen.

On our arrival in New York, Aunt Ada took an apartment for us in the center of the city on Thirty-sixth Street near Broadway, accessible to the theatres. Our daily routine began. Every morning I studied and in the afternoon went through my parts in our little drawing room, dressed in a gown with a train so that later on I might be free and unhampered in movement and gesture. Aunt Ada held the prompt book and read all the other parts. I acted my roles in the last degree of detail, since I knew it might be long before I could get a public hearing. Indeed no time was set for the end of my period of study. No matter how long it should take to accomplish my ambition, I was prepared to wait and work.

In addition to my Shakespeare, my library now consisted of Webster's unabridged dictionary, an encyclopedia, Shelley, Keats, Browning, Sir Walter Scott, Burns. Whenever I was in the slightest doubt as to any sound, I consulted my dictionary and practiced as a singer practices his notes, giving attention to vowels and final consonants. I must have distinct utterance, a clean enunciation. To pronounce correctly, I must study words —words—words.

Day after day Aunt Ada rehearsed me in our little flat. What a stumbling block was Sheridan Knowles's play, *The Hunch-*

back—the scene where Julia makes her first entrance with Helen into the garden. The mood of Helen is one of irritation with country life, and Julia is laughing at her. As I conceived the entrance, I had planned to be heard laughing offstage before I entered.

Aunt Ada, always very gentle with me, said, "Let us pause awhile. I do not think your laugh is mirthful enough. It sounds forced and unconvincing."

To that I agreed and answered, "I find it exceedingly difficult to do. Shall I try it again?"

Repeatedly I tried it but failed to satisfy either of us. Discouraged, I pleaded, "Aunt Ada, show me how to do it."

"Oh, no," she refused and wisely told me, "If I show you how to do it, you will do it as I do it, not as you would do it."

Therefore I redoubled my efforts to get the business as I knew it should be. Not that day nor for several days did it come to me. Meantime I practiced my laughter—as I had done for the part of Maria—in Central Park during my daily walk, or wherever else I might be unnoticed, and eventually I conquered and laughed with mirth.

So it went in all my work with Aunt Ada, her system being to let me evolve the appropriate expression from my own understanding, she standing by as critic. She had been a stock-company actress for many years and had seen the plays we were rehearsing performed by various women. We had long conferences on the wisdom or propriety of certain points being treated in special ways, and I was always left to decide what I should prefer to do. Thus I cultivated my judgment, my invention.

My day's work for some years consisted of rising at an early hour, eating a light breakfast and taking the horsecar to Central

Park, where I explored every nook and cranny. In those days the park was not crowded, especially at an early morning hour, and I would go through my entire role aloud without restraint or interruption, practicing mirth or whatever emotion the character dictated. That would take nearly two hours after which I returned home to have my luncheon with Aunt Ada and begin the afternoon routine. I, having donned my gown with the train, would push the furniture aside, arrange it for the scenes, and proceed, Miss Dow sitting off in the corner holding the book and reading the other parts. I invariably found her encouraging and usually satisfied, although I was not always pleased myself. For days at a time I was gloomy about my progress and felt I was not improving. Then all of a sudden the time would come when after infinite pains I would achieve the effect desired.

In the evening I would go to the theatre if something were being played which I thought might be instructive. All this time every working hour, every minute of every hour, seemed to me wasted unless it contributed something to my purpose. The emphasis of every word was weighed, considered and determined; nothing was left to chance. I dared not assume I possessed genius. Reading the lives of the great actors, I perceived that without their indefatigable labor they would never have achieved.

With Aunt Ada's help I made prompt books of *Romeo and Juliet, Twelfth Night, Ingomar, The Hunchback, Pygmalion and Galatea,* and *The Lady of Lyons,* including the business for all the characters, most of it new and original. Consequently I was prepared after three years' application to conduct rehearsals without a glance at the books of those six plays. I not only knew every word and gesture of my own part but those of every other part.

Old actors have frequently declared that it was impossible for a novice to have so complete a conception of plays without long and laborious experience. What they meant, no doubt, was that such careful preparation was unusual. Yet it is a familiar fact that opera singers are usually prepared in the music, words and stage business of a number of operas before they make their bow.

Enter now my second great benefactor, a man who was in fact a chief reason for Aunt Ada's taking me to New York. Stage directions for his appearance in my life might read: *Thunder and lightning. Alarums and excursions. Enter Professor Price.*

chapter 3

"What's in a Name?"

Parson Price had been a professional singer of high repute, a pupil of the noted teacher, Garcia, in London before he came to America. He had studied under Garcia for the express purpose of becoming an expert in vocal instruction. His was an excellent tenor voice, and in the stock-theatre days he was employed to sing between the acts. Being a Welshman he was extremely careful, almost to an exaggerated degree, with the enunciation of double l's and double d's.

One night in Scranton, Pennsylvania, when I was in Josephine Reilly's company, I had played the part of Balthazar in *Romeo and Juliet*. Mr. Price, who had been attending the Welsh *Eisteddfod* celebration in town, came behind the scene to renew his former friendship with Aunt Ada. I was presented to him as her protégée, ambitious to play the great roles. In his hearty way he clapped me on the shoulder and said, "When you come to New York, we must try conclusions with your voice."

I remembered his words one day in New York when Aunt Ada was rehearsing me in the part of Juliet, the balcony scene.

As a child my voice had been forced and the chest tones greatly emphasized, detracting from the medium register. Now I realized my serious handicap because Juliet's lines in the balcony scene must be uttered with great delicacy. Her tones must

be young, ardent, penetrating to the uttermost part of the theatre—a feat of no small difficulty, for the scene is one of tender
confidence, of low tones, of apprehension of discovery, of fear
of fatal consequences. Juliet scarcely breathes her words to herself and to the night. Clear enunciation, a great variety of tone,
and a flexible voice are absolutely indispensable to a really fine
performance.

I was woefully aware that my voice was inadequate and in
despair I begged Aunt Ada, "Can't I go to Professor Price? He
said he'd help me."

That was the request my mentor had hoped and planned I
would make.

Next morning we hastened to the professor's studio in West
Seventeenth Street, a third-floor-rear apartment. On his door
was a placard which read: *Beware! Pedlars not allowed.* As
we mounted the stairs, we heard a quavering tenor voice practicing scales. Tones soared skyward until we felt the singer
must lose the top of his head. Those exercises were interspersed
with violent rebukes in Welsh and English—chords loudly
struck on the piano—shouts of "Go on! Do it! I tell you to
do it!" The poor wretch within appeared to be straining every
nerve in desperation, as a horse might in attempting to take a
hurdle under whip and spur.

We waited for a moment of silence, not daring to enter or
even knock until the racket subsided. At length we timidly
tapped. A voice roared, "Come in!" The man who had been
singing was preparing to depart, somehow unscathed by all he
had undergone. He bowed—the top of his head still was on—
and he went his way.

Professor Price rushed forward, greeting us with exuberant amiability, a total change of demeanor.

"Let us get ready," he cried at once, seating himself at the piano. Aunt Ada retired to a corner, and I took my stand in the middle of the room. The professor arrested an attack on the piano to shout, "Take off that bonnet."

Obeying, I began "Do—re—mi," while he led the way on his instrument. He broke off abruptly, strode toward me and tugged at my collar.

"Here! Loose this. How can you ever vocalize with your throat fastened up like this?"

Rather perturbed, I undid my collar. He went back to the piano and began again. My voice was tested in every conceivable tone for about twenty minutes. I was then invited to sit down and rest. "Now let's talk," said the professor.

I explained about the balcony scene, and he understood perfectly and asked me to read it.

When I finished his face became more solemn and finally he said, "I can't say yet that I can help. It will take patience on my part and great industry on yours, my child." He shook me by the shoulder. "I find you have no medium tones. After two or three months of lessons I can better tell. At the end of that time we'll let Miss Dow hear what we have done. More than that I cannot say at this time."

Ignorant of the difficulties to be overcome but determined to conquer, I answered, "I will try."

The professor explained, "We will have to make a middle register. We must make one. Perhaps we can do it, if you will do your part." Then, turning to Aunt Ada, who understood music, he said, "In order to make the middle register we must take from the chest and the head tones, nourish and feed the middle register from them. She is still so young. It may possibly be done."

Aunt Ada suggested one lesson a week.

"Three. She must have three. She must come three times a week," the teacher insisted.

Aunt Ada protested that the expense would be greater than we could afford. Professor Price looked at me. He made a queer grimace. I must have had a prayer in my eyes.

"We will talk of that some other time," said he.

For three years he received no money, nor did he ask for any, nor could he know whether he would ever receive any.

Not until, after long struggle, I had vindicated his trust could I pay him what he had so richly earned. My true debt to him I can never pay.

For three months I practiced daily, one hour in the morning, one in the afternoon—scales, exercises. I wonder we were not requested to leave our flat. That daily labor did not interfere in the least with my long rehearsals with Aunt Ada, my work on the prompt books, my long walks in the park, my constant thought of my roles. Three times a week I went to the studio and underwent the always exciting experience of my lessons.

"I can't do any more," I would cry.

"Oh, yes, you can," the professor said sternly. "Let's have one more go at it. Now then, sustain that note. Make it fine, round and full. Sustain it! I will punish you! Sustain it!!!"

"I can't. I have no more breath."

"Why not? What's the matter? The room's full of breath. The world's full of breath. Again!"

When I failed, I submissively listened to his scoldings in English and Welsh. I am sure the Welsh was swearing and that he was consigning me to the mercy of ancient Druids who practiced human sacrifice. When I ascended scales, he spurred me on. "Come on! Now. Do it, do it, or I will punish you!" he shrieked, rising up out of the piano stool with his fingers still on the notes. If I pleased him he would nod his head, smile, beckon me to a seat beside him and sing some gay snatch of song, while I sat panting.

"Tell Aunt Ada we have done well today," he praised. "Next time fetch her with you."

The great day had arrived!

We went through our exercises as usual. The professor was even more exuberant, more excitable than usual. He berated, cajoled me, scolded me, threatened. "Do it! Do it, or I will punish you."

For the hundredth time in those three months I intoned:

> "Two souls with but a single thought.
> Two hearts that beat as one . . ."

on every note for two and a half octaves, sustaining vowel sounds, careful of final consonants. At every imaginable pitch I intoned:

> "Glory be to the Father and to the Son
> And to the Holy Ghost."

"Drop the jaw! Open the mouth—wider—wider! Stand on your toes. Now we're at it. *Now* we're coming to it. It's coming! It's coming!" He chanted with me, banging the chords, bobbing his head, half out of his seat:

"As it was in the beginning—is now
and ever shall be—world without end."

"The child can do it!" the professor shouted jubilantly. He
kissed me, gave me a great hug which lifted me from the floor.
"The child can do it!" he repeated and added more calmly,
"With her patience and her capacity for work, that girl can do
anything in the world she wants to do."

My aunt smiled and nodded.

So it was settled that I should continue my lessons three
times a week as long as Professor Price lived. Whenever I was
in New York, I took a daily lesson from him, no matter what
the demands on my time might be.

I have always been happy that his creation of my voice
opened for him a new branch of vocal instruction. Previously
he had confined himself to training singers. Now he could
coach speakers. Clergymen, who had seen my performances on
the stage, went to him to improve their delivery. I have been
told that mothers took their daughters to him, asking that he
make their voices like Julia Marlowe's.

Professor Price invariably replied to each, "Oh, madam, I
did not make Julia Marlowe's voice. God made it."

But Julia Marlowe answers, "God gave Julia Marlowe the
will to concentrate, to labor. But Parson Price showed me the
road, and I declare that he is responsible for my voice."

For a while Professor Price tried to persuade me to become
a singer. He was of the opinion that, with my training as an
actress, I would have an advantage, and that my voice would

become a powerful mezzo-soprano. But I was not to be weaned from my desire.

That the quality created by him has been of the greatest value to me as an actress, my critics have proclaimed with one accord. They did not credit me with beauty (no courtiers, those critics), but they admitted that the instrument of speech was a weapon I could wield with skill.

On one occasion Aunt Ada, having in mind perhaps the effect of passion produced in certain scenes by actors of an older time, sensed some lack in my early efforts, and urged me to put more strength into a certain passage, more volume of voice. Concerned, I told Professor Price, asking him to help me to achieve that effect.

"What does Aunt Ada say?" he inquired.

"She said," I replied, "that she would like to come behind me and stick a hatpin into me to wake me up."

"Read the speech to me," he ordered.

I did so, as I felt and understood the scene.

"Aunt Ada is wrong," said he. "If you do what she suggests, you will tear your voice to tatters, and we shall destroy that for which we have struggled all these months."

Acting on his advice, which I never failed to remember during a long career, I managed to maintain the freshness of my voice under exceedingly trying circumstances—when I was playing heavy tragic roles eight times a week.

Sound is too frequently mistaken for passion. It may be remarked here that the curse in *King Lear* and that in *Les Horaces* were delivered by Garrick and Rachel, respectively, with such low intensity that they became doubly appalling. Those two speeches rank high among the passionate utterances in drama.

Professor Price was one of the most admirable characters I have ever met, and my obligation to him is infinite. He was a most humorous and delightful creature. His ideals were high, his enthusiasm unbounded, his impulses sudden and on occasion overwhelming. His assumption of anger and descents into comedy were startling and disconcerting to anyone not familiar with his Welsh effervescence.

One day I was singing with much feeling to his touching accompaniment:

> "Oh, loving heart, trust on, trust on.
> One true heart beats for you alone.
> Oh heart, trust on, trust on.
> Oh, loving heart, trust on!"

The professor's eyes were closed, his head swaying with ecstasy.

In the midst of it the door opened, and there appeared the bushy, black head of a burly man, his arms full of feather dusters. He extended the dusters toward us and, with a smile which displayed a great many teeth, he murmured something beseeching in a foreign tongue.

An awful moment of silence ensued. "Pedlars!" almost screamed the professor, and he sprang from his piano stool, gathering up sheets and books of music and hurling them at the duster man's bushy head. The latter yelped, dashed for the stairs and fled, leaping several steps at a time. The professor followed at his heels, hurling scores and shouting imprecations in Welsh, a language to be commended to anyone wishing to terrify an intruder. Pursued and pursuer disappeared down the stairs amid a wild conglomeration of sound, the Welshman's yells, the foreigner's shrieks. I leaned over the balustrade in fear of a tragedy. A line from Shakespeare ran through my mind and never had one seemed more apt to the occasion. Certainly at this moment I could declare with Hotspur:

Now I perceive that the Devil understands Welsh.

Shortly the professor came up the stairs, whistling, calmly seated himself at the piano and, with a nod of his head and a smile, began the accompaniment. And once more I sang of a "loving heart."

One of my favorite exercises consisted of a song which necessitated careful breathing and the ability to hold certain notes while the dramatic musical accompaniment, as it were, worked up the agony. This matter of proper scientific breathing was one of our most important studies. The knowledge of how to fill the lower portion of the lungs and to sustain with power a long note is one of the most vital accomplishments for both singer and actor. Madame Bernhardt relates that she was able slowly to declaim a speech of four Alexandrines with delicately shaded emphasis without taking a breath.

The song in question was called "The Two Letters"; its piano accompaniment was elaborate and Wagnerian in volume. Both the professor and I girded our strength for it, as much as to say to each other, "Now we'll show what we can do."

> A maiden sat upon a cliff,
>   As fair as fair can be.
> Her face was pale and oft she cried,
>   "Ah woe! Ah woe to me!"

Two tear-stained letters open lay—
    One old, the other new.
It was the old, the oft-told tale
    Of lovers false and true.
"O! darling mine," the letter old began.
"Have faith in me whate'er betide.
Come weal or woe I live alone in thee
I live alone in thee.

"They say that you are lowly born
    And I am proud and high,
But never fear love levels all.
    The world I scorn—defy."
"One year ago," the maiden sighs,
    "He won my heart. Today
He bids me to forget him. Forget him?

"Do sun and moon forget to shine?
My breath he was and, taking that,
There's nothing left but death—ah-h-h"

                              (*She screams*)

The maiden rose, with arms aloft,
She sprang into the sea.
And far was heard that piteous cry—
"Have mercy, God, on me.
Have mercy, God, on me!"

As the maiden sank beneath the waves, the piano thundered
under the professor's dancing hands. His voice vied with mine.
Every nerve in his rather small, stout body seemed to be quiver-

ing with intensity and excitement. He banged the keyboard,
lifted himself out of his seat and when I reached the great climax,

There's nothing left but death.   (*Scream*)

he half rose and raised one arm in the air, his blazing glance
daring me not to take the high note on "Forget him?" Actually
screaming the words in unison with me, he would cry, as with a
gesture of despair I prepared to plunge beneath the waves,
" 'Forget him!' Keep it up! On the toes—mouth open—chest
out. Now come on, come on, 'Forget him?' " His hair stood
on end, his eyes distended. " 'Forget him!' Damn him! Now
then up! up!"

"Do sun and moon forget to shine?"

"Get ready now! On the toes!"

"There's nothing left but death!"

A great scream from both of us.

"The maiden rose, with arms aloft
She sprang into the sea."

We plunged over the cliff. The piano thundered. The waves
overwhelmed us.

"Mouth open. I will scold you. I will punish you. Do it! Do
it!"

"Have mercy, God, on me
Have mercy, God, on me."

More thunder from the piano. The professor, his eyes on the ceiling, his feet on the pedals, rapt, ecstatic, his body swaying, pounded out a grand finale. He bounded up, hugged me. "Good! Splendid!" Welsh exclamations. "We are doing well. We are doing well!"

My insistence that my voice became a valuable instrument may savor of vainglory. But I had not been born with a voice of gold or a well-stored mind or a beautiful face. When I look back at a photograph of Fancy Brough when she was eighteen, I feel it belongs in Portia's leaden casket.

So only by infinite endeavor could I make a career for myself on the stage—in the theatre I loved. By hard study with Aunt Ada, by my voice training with Professor Price, I built and crossed my first bridges. The toil of their building took three long years. But without them, like the maiden in the song, I would have plunged into a sea of obscurity and sunk beneath the waves.

At last it was time to give thought to a name, a name that might someday head programs and be written large on billboards.

"What's in a name?" Juliet asked. For an actor or actress, the answer could be made, there is a great deal.

Sarah Frances Frost was far too ominous a label for my great adventure. What should I call myself? It was true that we had outlived the day when to be an actor was to disgrace one's family tree, be it never so humble. Stage names and pen names can be the refuge of the timid, but in the theatre men and women use their own names when they are euphonious. Mine, however, would invite the wandering wits to do their worst. "Frost!" I could hear them. "Wasn't she one!"

Fancy Brough then? No. I had used it with the Cincinnati company, but somehow I could no longer accept it.

I took up my dictionary and went through the alphabetical list of names, ancient and modern, Christian and Pagan. For a day I called myself Mistress Bellamy, the name of a great actress long gone. Delving into the significance of names I made this list:

> Rosina . . . . Beautiful as a rose
> Eulalia . . . . Fair speech
> Camilla . . . . Attendant at a sacrifice
> Beatrice . . . . Making happy
> Penelope . . . . A weaver
> Ophelia . . . . A serpent
> Rosamund . . . . . . Famous protector

Diana and Chloe seemed too fantastic, Ruth and Esther too Biblical. I was Roberta Tennyson for a while, but soon abandoned that. Camilla tempted me but sounded too much like the flying trapeze. I shuddered at Montmorency, Fitzgerald, De Vere and Molyneux. "Will you have *me*, lady?" they seemed to say with Don Pedro. And I replied with Beatrice, "No, my lord! unless I might have another for working days. Your lordship is too precious to wear every day."

I had become enamored of Juliet, but it appeared to suggest the diminutive. Julia, heroine of *The Hunchback*—there was a brave and witty girl. The name began to ring in my ears. "Julia!"

So much for a first name—now the last. Through my head ran Shakespeare's tribute to his fellow Elizabethan, Christopher Marlowe:

Dead Shepherd! now I find thy saw of might.
Who ever loved that loved not at first sight? *

Marlowe! That was it. Julia Marlowe. The name had dignity
and a musical lilt.

Fancy Brough looked at herself in the glass and considered
herself as Julia Marlowe. Yes, it would do wonderfully if I
worked hard enough to do it honor.

"Good-bye, my Fancy," said I.

At once I began instructing my colored maid, Celia, on my
change of name.

"Celia," said I, "from today on I shall be known as Julia
Marlowe. I am no longer Sarah Frances Frost nor am I Fancy
Brough. People will ask, 'Is Miss Marlowe at home?' or say
'Please deliver these flowers to Miss Marlowe' or 'I have come
to try on Miss Marlowe's new costumes' or 'May I have the
pleasure of an interview with Miss Marlowe?' Do you understand, Celia?"

"Lawdy, Miss Frances," said Celia, "you don't want to call
yoself Julia! Why I'se known lots of trashy gals calls theirselves
Julia. I suttinly hopes you won't call yoself dat, Miss Julia."

But I would, and the die was cast. From that day Julia Marlowe I became.

* *As You Like It.* Act III, Scene 5. An allusion to Marlowe who died in 1593,
six years before Shakespeare's comedy was written. The "saw" is quoted from
Marlowe's *Hero and Leander.*

chapter 4

"With That Nose?"

Three years of careful preparation for the stage and of voice training lay behind me. I had rechristened myself with a name I hoped to make famous. Now what parts should Julia Marlowe play? I never had any doubt of the answer. The great roles of Shakespeare.

I knew that Mary Anderson, Adelaide Neilson, Fanny Kemble, and other actresses before me had adopted my plan of campaign and made their bows as Shakespearean heroines, and I was ready to try to follow in their footsteps. So, supported by Aunt Ada, I took my courage in both hands and sallied forth to seek opportunity.

First we called at the old Lyceum on Fourth Avenue near Twenty-third Street and requested an interview with Daniel Frohman, the manager of that theatre and director of Madame Modjeska's tours. My hope in approaching Mr. Frohman was that since he had given up the management of Madame Modjeska who had retired temporarily, he might be interested in placing me before the public in the roles I had been studying. I had no idea of considering minor parts. I was determined to begin at the top of the ladder and firmly believed I was equal to it.

Aunt Ada and I were shown up to Mr. Frohman's private office, a very small, low room in the front part of the theatre over the entrance hall. There was barely enough space for a large roller-top desk and two or three chairs. Aunt Ada told my story and asked the manager if he had the time to hear me read.

How deeply that interview is imprinted on my memory! So often afterwards girls and boys came with the same request to me. I looked back then on the slim girl of eighteen whose heart beat high with hope and never refused to listen. Many a time after a long performance I sat on the dim stage and heard them read—very seldom well. Knowledge that long preparation is necessary never has been brought home to most youngsters who aspire to a career in the theatre. Though criticisms were not always taken in good part, and I wasn't sure they would bear any fruit, I listened and encouraged so far as I could. For I always saw young Julia Marlowe standing in their place looking for a chance.

Mr. Frohman was polite but plainly indifferent. A girl wishing to begin as a star was no novelty to him. Still he was patient and waved me to begin.

The space was so small that I was at some disadvantage, but I was not nervous. I felt quite sure of the scenes which I had rehearsed so many hundred times in every detail.

"I will read the ring scene and the scene with Orsino from *Twelfth Night*," I announced. "That scene contains the lovely speech, 'She never told her love.'"

When I finished, Mr. Frohman said without enthusiasm, "Very nice—very nice." Being familiar with the play, he must have had comparisons in mind, odious ones no doubt.

Yet, as a kind man, he felt called upon to offer some noncommittal criticism. When a person reads, well or ill, some sort of conversation must ensue; one can't discuss the weather nor immediately indicate the door. I smiled encouragingly, hoping I had made an impression.

It was my business in the ring scene the manager chose to criticize when I came to the lines: "How will this fadge?* My master loves her dearly," I indicated "my master" on the thumb of my left hand with the forefinger of my right hand and I indicated "her" on the first finger.

"And I, poor monster"—I pointed to my second finger—"fond as much on him; and she"—once more first finger—"mistaken seems to dote on me"—again my second finger—"What will become of this?"

Here Viola gave up the problem with discouragement.

That piece of business subsequently amused audiences and never failed to draw gentle laughter. But Mr. Frohman questioned it.

"Don't you think you make a mistake in indicating the characters by that business on your fingers?" he asked.

"Why?"

"It rather looks as if you thought the audience wouldn't understand unless you did that. You should give them credit for a little more intelligence."

Mr. Frohman held a high opinion of audiences or perhaps feared that my business might recall that of Lord Dundreary when he puzzled his brains over the relative positions of his mother and his brother Sam in a certain family problem.

"That's Sam," says his lordship. "That's Sam's mother. No. *That's* Sam's mother—that's *my* mother." (His finger, the second, will not remain erect.) "Hang it," says Dundreary, "my mother won't stand up! I never had such a fool of a mother as

* Prosper.

that." (Much brain-racking.) "That's one of those things that no fellah can find out."

Or it may be that Mr. Frohman, feeling that some remark not altogether demolishing was in order, took the kindly course of an old actor I have heard of who, when approached by the anxious proprietor of a small hotel asking if the dinner was satisfactory, replied with enthusiasm, "Delightful! Delightful, my boy! The pepper's excellent."

Mr. Frohman suggested that I might be willing to play in his stock company, but I felt I would be hampered in such work. I should have to play any parts assigned me and wait years to reach my goal, with no chance to play Shakespeare. When I declined, Mr. Frohman glanced at the door as though considering what a very nice door it was—what a particularly convenient door for the exit of a girl who wanted to begin as a star.

The girl took the hint and went her way, not a tiny bit discouraged. She realized the fight would be a long one. Had she not watched such struggles since she was a child of ten—seen scant audiences with slack interest watch the efforts of accomplished actors?

But the plays! The plays! Surely their beauty and humanity must appeal to others as they had to her. Her well-thumbed volume of Shakespeare, purchased with a child's pocket money, had opened for her a world of delight. The heroines were living creatures who possessed her and for whom she must fight.

We next approached J. M. Hill at the Union Square Theatre. He was the manager of Margaret Mather who had recently appeared with success in *Romeo and Juliet* but was rumored to have severed her connection with him. We therefore thought he might be willing to consider me.

Aunt Ada proposed that I should read Mr. Hill the balcony scene from *Romeo and Juliet.*

When I finished, Mr. Hill let us understand he considered himself an authority on that scene, having instructed Miss Mather in it.

"You have conceived the scene in far too light a manner," he pronounced. "You are almost flippant, too coquettish. It should be played in a heavier way. More sombre tones." Thereupon he bowed us out, saying, "Let me have your address. Perhaps you'll hear from me later." How many aspirants have heard those words! How often has the postman been watched for and in vain!

"Heavier! More sombre!" Mr. Hill as a manager was informed on the balcony scene, but his was not my idea of Juliet, a girl of fourteen.

LADY CAPULET: Thou know'st my daughter's of a pretty age?

NURSE: Faith, I can tell her age unto an hour.

LADY CAP: She's not fourteen.

Should the tender beauty of a girl's first confession of love be heavy, sombre? Never! "Like softest music to attending ears."

I was puzzled but strong in my convictions. Shakespeare himself had rehearsed the boy who originally played Juliet. I wondered what that boy was like. Was it true, as I had read somewhere that sometimes the performance at the Globe was delayed while Juliet was shaved? No, the boy must have been young, perhaps a mere child, like one of our choir boys.

To the efforts of managers, trying to discourage my ambition, a successful actor added his bit.

One day I met Henry Dixey, who was playing at the Bijou Theatre in a great hit, the travesty *Adonis*. I was introduced to him as "a young lady who is going to play all the great parts in Shakespeare." Mr. Dixey looked me over in a lordly fashion and delivered a scathing comment.

"With that nose?" asked Mr. Dixey.

It was something of a shock, for I had not till then considered my nose a handicap. Having ready no argument in favor of my nose, I let the matter drop, but as soon as I reached home I ran to the looking glass.

Adelaide Neilson had a nose like mine, I assured myself. Coquelin has a nose tilted even more heavenward. Rejane has a small nose; Ellen Terry's nose certainly is not a big one. William Pitt's was insignificant. Michelangelo may truly have had a nose of dimensions but managed to get along after it had been reduced to a certain flatness. Socrates had a small nose, even a "pug." Diogenes certainly did not boast of his. I had not yet heard of Cyrano's nose, or I should have considered that a nose of such grandeur was more disastrous than none at all.

The point was: What sort of a nose was Juliet's or Rosalind's?

Surely noses young and fair. I thought of Bardolph's nose, which Falstaff said lighted him the way o' dark nights from tavern to tavern. I watched noses in the street and divided them into categories: comic, tragic, noses of hope or despair.

At length I contented myself with my own and determined to follow it. Sooner or later I would follow it to Shakespeare.

Aunt Ada and I now felt that other New York managers would hardly be interested in casting me in roles for which I had prepared myself. I would have to manage myself and give a performance to show what I could do. But such a project must be financed.

I had not seen my mother for three years. She had remained in Cincinnati, superintending her home and attending to her lodginghouse. Always extremely frugal, supporting her family, she had practiced the doctrines she preached to us, "Take care of the pennies and the pounds will take care of themselves." I, like all children, had sometimes found that a wearisome creed and had chafed at my limited pocket money. But now in my need, how my mother's thrift was vindicated. When Aunt Ada told her that a public performance must be my next step but that we could not finance it, my mother at once volunteered to provide the money from her savings. She had been impressed by my industry and devotion to the cause I had at heart. From her came the thirteen hundred dollars we needed.

A two-week tour of small towns in New England, beginning in New London, was arranged. After that, if my performances warranted it, I would give a matinee in New York. I was to open as Parthenia in *Ingomar* and also play Galatea in *Pygmalion and Galatea* and Pauline in *The Lady of Lyons*. I made my own clothes for the parts of Parthenia and Galatea. The intricacies of Pauline's wardrobe were beyond me, so those costumes were purchased.

Now the time arrived when the maid Celia did indeed open the door of our flat and hear the predicted words: "I have come to try on the costumes for Miss Julia Marlowe."

I stood before the mirror in Pauline's brave attire looking

far into the future, ready to walk through the looking glass into Wonderland.

It was May, 1887. My company was recruited from the many actors who trod the pavements of Union Square. Many in those days were experienced in what was called the "legitimate repertoire." One could easily pick up a cast for one or all of the plays of Shakespeare and of other dramas.

It was then the custom for an actor to supply his own wardrobe, and that was part of his assets when he sought engagements. Scenery to meet every emergency was kept in stock by theatres everywhere. A new theatre would be at once equipped with sets for every contingency: a palace, a forest, a cottage, a sea coast, back drops which would carry one from pole to pole were at the disposal of all comers. Audiences of those palmy days were glad to welcome year after year the familiar canvases —a happy time for the pockets of adventurous spirits. Therefore for such as I there was little advance expenditure. We engaged our "troupe," or as one proud exponent of the drama poetic had it on his playbills, our "coterie" of players. We bought our railway tickets. We arrived in the town where we were to open our engagement. We stepped upon the stage and played our parts.

My company rehearsed in the Bijou Theatre, New York. My prompt books, made with such minute care, were in charge of Aunt Ada who directed rehearsals. Of course I knew all the characters in all the plays—their every action, their very thoughts, all gestures, inflections, positions, movements in every scene. I needed no book. My head, my heart, were full of them. For three years I had lived with them to the exclusion of all other associates. In all my walks, at meals, these people of the imagination had been my companions. Now they took on flesh at last. Our rehearsals were swift and precise. The actors were considerate and willing. All promised well.

When we reached New London, I saw that I was billed in huge letters on posters as "The Beautiful Young Actress, Julia Marlowe." Please believe I was not guilty of that. Such attacks on the credulity of the public are perpetrated by the joyous hands of advance agents. "The Beautiful Young Actress." I could hear a sardonic echo from Mr. Dixey: "What! with that nose?"

When our forces assembled that Sunday night, we discovered that one member, an old man who was to play Myron, Parthenia's father, was missing. We could take no chances, so we telegraphed to New York for another actor, prepared in the three roles required. Promptly an experienced old gentleman arrived.

Aunt Ada and I were walking toward the theatre in company with William E. Beach, my leading man, when we met our new recruit. Mr. Beach knew him. The new member, evidently a survival of the "old school" and blessed with considerable manner but down on his luck, walked ahead with Aunt Ada.

Said Mr. Beach in low tones, "That is old Pope Cook."

"You know him?" I asked.

"Surely, he's not going to play Myron. He's too old."

"But Myron is an old man," I protested. "He is my father."

"But not your great-grandfather."

"But he does not look very old. How old is he?"

"Why, he's so old—you'll see when he begins to act how old he is. Why, he's so old he could have posted bills for Roscius upon the Appian Way."

This certainly seemed a very extremity of age. But Mr. Pope belied the humorous Mr. Beach's pronouncement and played his part well.

The night came at last. The audience was small. "The beautiful young actress" was entirely unknown, and the trumpets of our advance man lured few people to the play. But that did not affect me at all. I was launched on my adventure and I was trying my wings. Many another night I was to face just such a scanty gathering, but always I was learning—learning—trying out on the stage what I had concluded to do in my own room, storing up in my eager mind experience for the victory of which I felt assured. I really felt like Longfellow's young man who bore the banner with the strange device, "Excelsior." I must not fail.

The performance went well; the few people present were enthusiastic. Next morning a critic on one of the local papers proclaimed in a line I'll never forget, "This young actress will climb the 'Diamond Ladder of Fame.' " The diamond ladder! A glittering prospect indeed! Other papers also gave me great encouragement. I clipped all the reviews and pasted them in my scrapbook. Here was some tangible evidence that I was climbing rungs of that ladder.

Our next town was Natick, where the house amounted to only ten dollars. It made no difference to me. I lived in the future, and before those lonely souls I practiced for performances to come.

That same lack of confidence greeted us everywhere else. It

takes a long time to obtain the public's favor in a new venture. Audiences are not readily persuaded of the excellence of a new performer in the great roles, as I was well aware.

The poor houses reminded me of an occasion when I was playing in Miss Reilly's company. It was a bitter cold night, and the theatre in some small Western town was terribly cold, an ancient auditorium heated by a large stove near the orchestra. The few spectators, scattered here and there, were wearing their overcoats and shivering with cold. As the play dragged sadly along, all of a sudden a man exclaimed, "Say, folks! Let's get down there by the stove." A small round of applause greeted the sentiment, and down scampered the frozen ones from their various neighborhoods to the friendly warmth. It was like the lecture tour on which Mark Twain and Bret Harte met with so few admirers that Twain stopped in the middle of his reading and invited those present to step up on the platform and he would send out for drinks and read as they sat around the table, an invitation gladly accepted.

But Julia Marlowe could not have afforded such hospitality. Her funds were low, and the thirst of her patrons might have been "five fathoms deep."

Our two weeks' tour, although we did not pay expenses, proved to the satisfaction of Aunt Ada and myself that I could do what I had set out to do. My mother's thirteen hundred dollars was nearly exhausted, but we paid all obligations and returned to New York. I had learned a great deal, played three important parts, gained much confidence.

Five months passed. Time must be very old and footsore that he walks so slowly! It was decided that I should wait until the

New York season was well advanced before making my appearance in the metropolis.

In October all arrangements were made for me to open in *Ingomar* at the Bijou Theatre. My manager, Robert E. J. Miles, controlled that theatre.

My one performance, a matinee, was to be chiefly an invitation affair for managers, actors and gentlemen of the press. It was not likely that the paying public would be curious to see an unknown young woman in an old, familiar play. *Ingomar* had been performed by many women stars in recent years, but even in those days New Yorkers were not great patrons of the legitimate. I myself saw Edwin Booth play at the Fifth Avenue Theatre to many empty seats. It was novelty New York liked—farce, melodrama, burlesque, variety. I hoped only to obtain a hearing, a favorable verdict, and then to tour the country.

There was just enough of my mother's contribution left to cover this one performance. The expense consisted only of one day's salaries for the cast. No printing was necessary.

An entirely new company was secured, for those who had supported me on my little tour were scattered far and wide.

Frank Evans, an actor of experience, was engaged to play Ingomar, and capable people filled the other parts. Many of them were appearing currently in other plays. Rehearsals were few, scenery was hurriedly borrowed from other theatres. Costumes were picked up by various actors here and there. The men wore Viking armor, with horns jutting from the helmets. Clothes mostly consisted of fur hides and rough cloaks of cloth. "Where did you get the door mats and the piano covers?" wrote one of our critics.

Except for my matinee day, the theatre housed the burlesque of *Adonis*, then in the midst of its great run of four hundred nights. All the associations of the place were allied with boisterous fun-making and pretty girls. Here I proposed to introduce a poetic drama, considered old-fashioned, stale and unprofitable. Yet I believed I could translate its ancient form into throbbing human experience. I felt sure of it. In any case this was the only chance I had. I seized it.

First rehearsals began in a perfunctory spirit. This company was a trifle more sophisticated than the earlier one. After all, I was only one of a long line of young women who had come to the stage ambitious to start at the top and often gravitating to the bottom. But before the end of a day's work, the interest shown by the cast made me feel that I was not to be classed with the failures which had gone before.

Finally came the night before the trial. I did not sleep much thinking of the morrow. As was my custom, I rose early, boarded a horsecar and went to Central Park. While I walked, I spoke all my lines and by noon returned to Thirty-sixth Street.

Aunt Ada, hoping to divert my thoughts a little from what was before me, took me to Trainor's Restaurant near the theatre and said, "Now, Fanny, choose what you want to eat."

"The prisoner arose and ate a hearty breakfast," I thought to myself, and my mind began to wander off to a criminal in the death cell. Why should he eat when the object of eating is merely to sustain the life soon to be taken from him?

"Poor man," I said aloud.

"Who?" said Ada.

"Why," said I, "the man who is to be hanged."

"What will you have to eat, Fanny?" she pressed.

I gazed absently at the bill of fare, where illimitable viands rendered a choice at any time a matter for reflection.

I thought of a lady I knew who, being overcome on an ocean

voyage, cried to a friend, "Oh! I am so sick. Get me a beefsteak and onions."

"That was funny," said I.

"What was?" said my aunt.

"Why, about the beefsteak and onions."

"Is that what you want?" she asked, surprise in her voice.

"Oh, no," I said. "I was just thinking."

A waiter approached us and regarded me hopefully.

They tell us that persons who are drowning are capable of minute observation. I was actually thinking of my part, and of the ordeal before me, and yet it worried me that the waiter's hands were not clean, that he had a button off his waistcoat, that he had not recently been shaved. I think he rather affected my appetite, and yet at any other time I might not have noticed him.

"He can't help it," said I.

"Help what?" said my aunt.

"The button," said I. "I suppose he has no time. I'll have some raw oysters," I ordered at last.

Raw oysters seemed nice and slippery and capable of reaching their destination quickly. I wanted to get away and be by myself. The noise, the people, the clatter seized my attention against my will.

Aunt Ada, an old stager, understood my mood and did not trouble me at this late hour with sympathy or advice. She herself had faced such ordeals. Between oysters I would say, "Do you think the critics will be there?" "Will the managers be there?" "Will the actors be there?" "I hope the actors will all think I do it well."

The curtain was to go up at two o'clock. It was about eleven. "I think I'll go now," said I.

"You have plenty of time," said Aunt Ada.

"I want to get there and sit still."

I picked up the small handbag which contained my wardrobe and my make-up. I was to wear only one costume, a simple woolen gown made by myself, some draperies of the same material, a ribbon to tie up my hair, a pair of sandals, some garlands of flowers. That was all. It was quite unnecessary for me to get to my dressing room so far in advance of the performance.

Nevertheless I had no fear. I have always considered that stage fright is due to unpreparedness. No, I had no stage fright. I have never had any.

I went to the stage door of the theatre and passed the stage-doorkeeper. Stage-doorkeepers are like weathercocks or thermometers and reflect the prosperity or adversity of their particular environment. This *Adonis* stage-doorkeeper oozed prosperity, but his look at me seemed to say, "Poor little thing." I fancy he included me among "those Shakespeare people" or "nuts." Perhaps he expected me to say, "By my halidom, the sun shines fair." He sighed and followed me to my dressing room, turned on the lights and left me to my thoughts.

No, I had no stage fright. I knew my moment would come if I were given half a chance—if the theatre did not catch fire or some other visitation of the unkind gods overwhelm me.

I had no dresser to intrude on my reflections. I unfastened my little bag. I arranged my dressing table. Soon I became Parthenia, the Grecian maid.

O, you theatre looking glasses! What secrets have you not surprised? What confident faces have you seen later stained with tears of disappointment? What should I see in my glass before the day was done?

How would the performance go? Accidents will happen

which can turn the best of efforts into ridicule. Dress rehearsals cost money; we had not been able to afford one. I had not been able to superintend the costumes. Their propriety had to be left to chance.

For the same reasons of economy there had been no rehearsal of the lights. A "light plot" had been handed to the gas man, and we were at his mercy. There would be no music to put our listeners in the mood of the tender scenes—musicians must be paid. The scenery was quite an unknown quantity, picked up here and there, and might or might not speak of ancient Greece. The savage Alemanni, whose wild shouts of rage or triumph were essential to the effect of several scenes were "supers" briefly instructed in their rather intricate duties.

The callboy announces "the half hour," then the first act. I take a hurried look at the stage, the scene seems sufficient. Aunt Ada is superintending. I leave all with confidence to her. I am standing in the wing in the upper entrance, for I go on a few lines after the curtain rises.

The curtain is up. There are many people in the entrances, but I see nobody. The place is Messaline. I am Parthenia. My mother speaks:

> The sun is nearly set, the city gates
> Will quickly close. Yet Myron comes not home.
> Parthenia too—wild girl! freed from her task
> Flies like a bird unfettered from her cage.
> (*She calls*)
> Parthenia! Daughter! Child!

I enter running. I kneel down beside my mother. There is some applause.

The first act of *Ingomar* gives Parthenia comparatively little opportunity except by way of introduction, so that I was not surprised that there was but slight applause when the curtain fell.

My first real opportunity came in the second act, when Parthenia, having surrendered herself to the savage followers of Ingomar, comes to his camp to offer herself as hostage for her father, who has been seized and made a slave.

Parthenia enters with several of the tribe; she stands on a slight eminence. On beholding her father a prisoner in chains she utters a piercing scream of joy. From that moment on the interest in the character of Parthenia increases. Her opportunities are rich for effective acting.

That scream was one of my most carefully thought-out effects. I had practiced it with my dear old teacher, Parson Price. We had decided upon the exact note, the precise volume, the duration, the accompanying movement and gesture. We had rehearsed it in his studio and on the stage. I had intended the scream to produce a precise effect, and on this day I could sense that I had succeeded splendidly.

The remainder of this second act of *Ingomar* consists in the subjugation of the Barbarian chief by the Greek maid. Thus:

INGOMAR: You must teach our women to weave such garlands.

PARTH: That is soon done. Thy wife
Herself shall soon weave wreaths as well as I.

INGOMAR: (*Laughs*) My wife—my wife—a woman—
Dost thou say?
I thank the Gods not I. This is my wife—
       (*Points to his accouterments*)

	My spear, my shield, my sword. Let him who will
	Waste cattle, slaves or gold to buy a woman;
	Not I. Not I.
PARTH:	To buy a woman?
	Bargain for wives
	As you would slaves. Buy them like cattle?
INGOMAR:	How do you in your city there?
PARTH:	Consult our hearts
	Love only buys us there.
INGOMAR:	Marry for love—what! do you love your hus-
	bands?
PARTH:	Why marry else?
INGOMAR:	What dost thou mean by love? What is it, girl?
PARTH:	'Tis of all things the most sweet,
	The life of Heaven—or so my mother says.

Later in the scene Ingomar says:

And now Parthenia tell me

  How that which you call love grows in the soul;
  And what love is. 'Tis strange but in that word
  There's something seems like yonder ocean fathomless.

Parthenia in a charming speech describes her ideal of love:

INGOMAR:	I never yet heard aught so beautiful
	But still I comprehend it not.
PARTH:	Nor I
	For I have never felt it! Yet I know
	A song my mother sang, an ancient song
	That plainly speaks of love at least to me.
	How goes it? Stay—

What love is if thou wouldst be taught
 Thy heart must teach alone,
Two souls with but a single thought,
 Two hearts that beat as one.

And whence comes love? Like morning's light
 It comes without thy call.
And how dies love? A spirit bright,
 Love never dies at all!

  (*Hesitates*)

INGOMAR: Go on!
PARTH: I know no more.
INGOMAR: (*Impatiently*) Go on, I say!
PARTH: Not now, I want more roses for my wreath.
  Yonder they grow, I will fetch them for myself.
  Take care of all my flowers and the wreath.
    (*Throws the flowers into Ingomar's
     lap and exits.*)

  (*Ingomar is left alone. He speaks to himself in
  deep abstraction.*)

Two souls with but a single thought,
Two hearts that beat as one.

The curtain falls.

On this occasion when Parthenia rushed from the stage in fear, the tumult of applause was so great it echoed and re-echoed in the theatre, and Ingomar could not be heard. He waited in vain for a chance to utter his lines, and at length the curtain was rung down. All I could hear was the thundering applause resounding about my head. The curtain went up and down—up and down. I stood on the stage and bowed again, and yet again. I was immeasurably happy but steadied by the thought that I had three more acts to come, each equally difficult.

The tumult lasted many minutes, long enough for many of the audience (as recorded in the papers next day) to go out and to return with arms full of flowers, and to throw them on the stage until the rude barbarian camp became a bower. I was kept busy lifting them up. These people, hardened theatregoers, unknown to me, were profoundly moved. Daniel Frohman, standing next to Mr. Miles at the back of the theatre, exclaimed, "Who would have believed it?"

Somehow I was not surprised. I had long primed myself for success; the only sense I had had was one of delay. I had accustomed myself to the idea of success and to that idea alone. It had never occurred to me that I could fail, and it was only the evidence of success that I had waited for.

But with the three acts still to come, I had not much time for reflection. The set remained unchanged, and again I was in the barbarian camp. To sketch the scene:

(*Ingomar overcome with his passion cries*)
INGOMAR: Didst thou not tell me once love was a fire?
          Parthenia, thou art mine.
PARTH: Ho! Stand off—away—(*Draws dagger*)
          Another step and I lie dead before thee.
INGOMAR: I am thy master.
          Girl, who art thou?
PARTH: Who am I? I am Parthenia,

Massilia's free-born daughter nourished
On a pure mother's breast, cradled in the arms
Of beauty and refinement, reared from childhood
In the holy service of the righteous Gods!
While thou—thou art the rude forest's outlaw
    son,
A savage—a barbarian—a cattle stealer.

INGOMAR: Darest thou?

PARTH: And now thou knowest who I am.
And who art thou? Thou art—

INGOMAR: —Now then by all the Gods I'll teach thee
How we treat our slaves—

PARTH: You tame them with the whip,
With hunger pain and thirst—but your slaves
                    love you not.
They only hate, despise as I do thee.

INGOMAR: Be silent or—

PARTH: No, for I scorn, deride thee—

INGOMAR: Thy life—

PARTH: Take it.

INGOMAR: (*Rushes at her, his sword drawn. He stops sud-
denly*)
No, no, I cannot.
Oh, I could tear myself, the world in pieces.
      (*Throws himself violently on the ground*)

The climax in the play when Parthenia cries, "Take it" had been formerly, with older actresses, a moment for great applause. But I had decided that it should be a moment of death-like stillness. It became so. The effect I achieved that day was precisely that I had planned—one could almost hear the silence. Such a tribute, when the situation warrants it, is more valuable to the play and to the player than hand clapping.

At the end of Act III, as with those succeeding, there were recalls and recalls.

At the close of the performance, Parthenia in his arms, Ingomar sighs:

> Two souls with but a single thought,
> Two hearts that beat as one.

The curtain fell, my ordeal was over. To applause, the curtain went up time after time. Many from the audience poured onto the stage to congratulate me with kind expressions of approval and some wonder too. One well-known journalist, A. C. Wheeler, known as "Nym Crinkle," took me by the shoulder and said solemnly, "My child, do you think that you are strong enough to do this?"

I laughed. I felt no fatigue. My cheeks were flushed with excitement. I had done what I knew I could do. I received all the compliments as if I had expected them, but I realized more than anyone there that I had only stepped up one rung of what my New London friend called "the Diamond Ladder of Fame."

My work for that day was done. . . .

One of George Meredith's characters says, "Why have I unfailingly succeeded? I never *doubted!* The world voluntarily opens a path to those who step determinedly." I never foresaw any hindrance from the first moment that it entered my head to be an actress when I was ten years old.

chapter 5

Juliet Bows

High commendation by the New York press followed the performance of *Ingomar*, and it was unanimous, the concensus being that something unusual had been accomplished. Julia Marlowe, the critics said, showed gifts of a high order, warranting the prediction of a great future.

The success of my matinee brought tempting offers from managers to act in modern plays, one from Steele Mackaye to play the leading part in *Paul Kauvar*. Here was certainty of large and secure remuneration and, for my years, a coveted position. But I brushed those proposals aside, for I had become a lover of beauty of speech, of high romance and glorious deeds, and Shakespeare was my goal. There is a line in one of George Meredith's books which says, "Who abandons Romance exchanges the sky for a ceiling." I would not consent to have my vision so limited. I preferred to keep my eyes upon the stars.

Someone defines poetry as "being glad about something and wanting others to experience that gladness." I really felt that way about Shakespeare's dramas. Their contemplation gave me extreme pleasure, and I was eager that others through me should share in my delight. I yearned to follow my recent success with *Romeo and Juliet* and *Twelfth Night*; Juliet and Viola were roles for which I had long been prepared. But how my next opportunity should come I had no idea.

What a blessed thing is youth, with its assurance of life and strength and its indifference to tomorrow! I had no money, yet I was convinced that my good angel was at this moment hovering over Thirty-sixth Street and would in time reveal himself.

One fine day he arrived in the person of H. E. Bristol, who ran a small restaurant on Sixth Avenue. He was an acquaintance of my manager, Mr. Miles, and had been invited to witness my performance as Parthenia. He was impressed to the point of being willing to invest five thousand dollars in my fortunes.

Mr. Bristol was a small, shy man, diffident and most polite. Sometimes Aunt Ada and I would dine with him at his restaurant and discuss our enterprise. When Henry E. Abbey, a manager, offered us a week at the Star Theatre, Mr. Bristol agreed to cover expenses.

Intervening weeks were spent in collecting my third company. I had decided to appear in *Romeo and Juliet*, *Twelfth Night* and *Ingomar*. My own costumes were ready made by a noted New York costumier. But although the materials were fine, after the usual theatrical fashion of that day little attention had been paid to correctness of period. So I obtained designs and pictures and remade all the costumes with my own hands. From my first appearances in the theatre I had been acquiring knowledge in designing theatrical costumes, and my experience in dressmaking when I was a little girl came to my assistance now.

In selecting my company, naturally the most important consideration was the leading man. As I studied the part of Juliet month after month, I had often wondered who my Romeo would be, and considering all available actors, I had set my mind on Joseph Haworth. I had seen him play in *The Moral*

Crime, a stirring play by Elwyn Barron, a dramatic critic of Chicago. The story resembled somewhat that of Sardou's *Fedora,* and Mr. Haworth's performance exhibited the very highest qualities of a romantic actor. I had seen him play also in *Denise* with Clara Morris at Daly's Theatre, a pronounced success. In appearance he somewhat resembled Edwin Booth. He was dark, with expressive eyes, a fine voice and really great tragic force. Also he played comedy lightly and charmingly. He was generally accounted at that time to be the best actor of leading roles on the American stage.

Aunt Ada made an appointment with Mr. Haworth to meet us at the Bijou Theatre and discuss an engagement. He had heard of the success of my performance of Parthenia and was at least curious enough to listen to a proposal. Yet the engagement was only for one week, and he was much in demand at the time.

Said Aunt Ada to Mr. Haworth, "Miss Marlowe is going to produce *Romeo and Juliet* at the Star Theatre on December the thirteenth."

Mr. Haworth looked at me, not unkindly.

"He will do it," I said to myself.

" 'Who aims at stars shoots higher far than he who means a tree,' " quoted Mr. Haworth. (I discovered later he carried about whole pockets full of aphorisms.)

"Yes," said Aunt Ada, "she is very ambitious."

"I am glad to hear it," approved Mr. Haworth. "I am ambitious myself. But Juliet is a good deal of an undertaking."

"He won't do it," I thought.

"They say that no woman can play Juliet until she has ceased to look like it," continued Mr. Haworth with his eyes on me.

"Miss Marlowe certainly would look Juliet." And he smiled at me as if to say, "That's a compliment."

"Oh! he's going to do it," said I to my heart.

"But," he went on, "the part really requires a lifetime of experience."

"No, he's not," I murmured and felt my cause was lost.

"We propose to produce *Romeo and Juliet, Twelfth Night,* and *Ingomar*," persisted Aunt Ada, who had a way of sticking to the matter in hand, "and the engagement would be for only one week."

"I have studied Romeo," Mr. Haworth said, "but I have not played the part. I would prefer to play Malvolio in *Twelfth Night*, but I am not up in it, and *Ingomar* would be a new part for me. Three new characters in one week. That's something of a task even for an experienced actor."

I felt my Romeo was giving excuses for not accepting the engagement, and I'm afraid I looked a little miserable.

"Let me think about it," temporized Mr. Haworth, preparing to go.

Aunt Ada stepped into the breech. "Why don't we go on the stage and run through the balcony scene?" she suggested. "That will give you some idea of what Miss Marlowe can do."

Mr. Haworth hesitated. He looked at his watch. I am sure he was about to say that he had an important engagement and, once he escaped, we probably would never see him again. His eyes fell on me, but I was praying with all my might that he would play Romeo and I was tongue-tied—I could not say a word in my own behalf.

"Very well," he granted. "Let us go through it."

The stage was cluttered with all sorts of lumber—furniture—

boxes—curious paraphernalia belonging to the burlesque of *Adonis*. A grand piano was surrounded by many chairs in one corner near the footlights where no doubt ladies of the chorus had that morning been taken through new songs. A poor, dim "tee light" shone sadly down in front. Ropes with sandbags at their ends hung from the flies.

It was late November, and the theatre was cold. Mr. Haworth shivered and turned up the collar of his overcoat.

"Shall we begin?" asked Aunt Ada.

On the instant, as if he had been waiting for that remark the whole night long, a man in some remote part of the stage began to hammer with all his might. Actors know something of the sort is bound to happen. It can't be explained, but must be accepted as inevitable and confronted with philosophy.

"I'll go and speak to him," volunteered Mr. Haworth and disappeared in the gloom.

Assisted by Aunt Ada, I moved some of the deal boxes to one side of the stage, placed them together and lifted a chair on top with its back facing the stage, so that I could lean on the balustrade of Juliet's balcony. Aunt Ada placed herself "within"— behind the boxes—so that she could speak the lines of the nurse.

The hammering had ceased. Mr. Haworth reappeared. "I don't see how we can manage it," said he skeptically. But he was not to escape.

"Oh, yes, this is the balcony," said I eagerly, "and that's the garden—there where you are now."

"Oh, I see," said Mr. Haworth with resignation. "Then I will enter from here," and he moved some of the *Adonis* properties to one side.

Romeo entered, listened to the derisive shouts of Mercutio and Benvolio and spoke, " 'He jests at scars that never felt a wound.' "

Four women cleaners, who had evidently been looking forward to this moment, commenced a violent argument and banged seats with violence.

"Ladies," protested Mr. Haworth. They paid no attention. "Ladies," shouted Romeo. They continued unmoved. Now Romeo addressed them more precisely at the top of his voice. "Cleaner-ladies," he cried.

There was a silence. "Are yez talking to us?" said one.

"I have that honor," replied Mr. Haworth, who had visited Ireland. "Will you, ladies, do me the great favor to remain silent while we go through a scene which I believe will give you very great pleasure? It is said to be the most exquisite love scene the world has ever known. You are women. Pray be seated in four of those chairs with your brooms on your knees. Let me beg that you will give us your attention while we wring your hearts. Do not restrain your tears."

The four "cleaner-ladies" subsided in four stalls.

Mr. Haworth began again:

> "He jests at scars, that never felt a wound.
> But, soft! what light through yonder window breaks?
> It is the east, and Juliet is the sun!
> Arise, fair sun, and kill the envious moon,
> Who is already sick and pale with grief,
> That thou her maid art far more fair than she:"

(Juliet enters on to the balcony)

"It is my lady; O, it is my love!
O, that I were a glove upon that hand,
That I might touch that cheek!"

I was no longer on a cluttered stage. I was in a garden of Verona. The little "tee light" became the moon in Italian skies.

"O Romeo, Romeo! wherefore art thou Romeo?"

Through the lines I was thinking: Oh, I wonder if I've said it well enough. Will he accept the engagement? Oh, I hope he will.

"Deny thy father and refuse thy name;
Or, if thou wilt not, be but sworn my love,
And I'll no longer be a Capulet."

Can he see my face in this darkness? I wondered. Do I look like Juliet? Will he get discouraged? How can I preserve any illusion under these circumstances?

I expected him to stop at the end of my line, but to my delight he went on:

"Shall I hear more . . ."
("Oh, yes," said my heart. "Please do.")
". . . Or shall I speak at this?"

Here, I knew, was a real, live Romeo. Previously those words had been spoken to me only by Aunt Ada. Now here was Romeo, dressed in a heavy winter overcoat, muffled up to the chin, on a cold dark stage, gazing up at me sitting on two deal boxes with a toppling chair. As the lines floated up to me, I heard them as, during three long years of preparation, I had imagined they must sound. His voice was beautiful, convincing. He had the rare quality of becoming at once the character he assumed. Romeo was never more real to me at any time in my life than that day.

The scene plays about twenty minutes. This thought came to me several times as I threw my heart into the lines: "He must think I am doing it well or he would stop." To my glad surprise he continued until the end.

"Parting is such sweet sorrow
That I shall say good-night till it be morrow."

"I'll do it!" shouted Mr. Haworth.

I hardly heard the comment of one of the cleaners, "This talk sets me crazy." Down I came from my dry-goods box and rushed to Aunt Ada, wondering if I had justified my apprenticeship of years, long years, wondering if I had really satisfied Mr. Haworth—wondering if I had done justice to Shakespeare. My anxiety was cut short by hearing Aunt Ada ask Mr. Haworth, "What is your salary?"

Alas, Romeo must have a salary!

Mr. Haworth descended from the clouds. "Oh, three hundred and fifty dollars a week," said he, and then with a very pleasant smile at me added, "But if it's any consideration, I'll take three hundred to play with Miss Marlowe."

I had never done much shopping and certainly none for Romeos, nor did I know their market values. But I thought it nice of Romeo to mark himself down like that, so I said gratefully, "Oh, Mr. Haworth!"

If he had said three million, it would have not seemed much to Juliet whose pocket had never in her life contained more than a few dollars at a time. There's nothing like beggary to make one generous. I quite expected a wizard to wave a wand and materialize the necessary money out of the air. However, to Juliet's aunt even three hundred dollars seemed a large sum. Still she was well aware of Mr. Haworth's value, and she jumped at the bargain.

The matter was settled. My Romeo was secured.

"Oh! it's fine," he said. "I'm full of enthusiasm about it. I'll go at once and start all the interest possible." He looked at me and intently for the first time—I mean at me, Julia Marlowe, for he had been gazing with love at Juliet. "We'll have a great success," he predicted and took my hand. "I'll be ready in a week for rehearsal—perfect, letter-perfect in my part."

He rushed through the dark auditorium and bowled over one of the cleaners who sat down hard on the floor. "A thousand pardons, madam," he cried as he lifted her up.

"The devil take ye!" was all his thanks, but Mr. Haworth embraced her and declaimed, " 'Look thou but sweet and I am proof against their enmity!' " Then once more waving his hand to me, he shouted, "It will be fine! It will be splendid!" and made his exit.

When rehearsals began, I found all the actors helpful and sympathetic. The first day I was regarded with curiosity, but my evident knowledge of what I was about soon inspired respect. There was no doubt nor hesitation over our stage directions. Everything proceeded swiftly and with certainty; every detail had been thought out.

"Seldom have I seen rehearsals go so smoothly," Mr. Haworth praised. He took pains to be kind and helpful, remaining after the others had gone to request that I go over scenes with him. He was a man of great experience and great natural gifts, and I owe much to his guidance.

Another instance of Mr. Haworth's exuberance occurred when one afternoon we went for a walk in Central Park after an early dinner to go through our lines. As dusk came on, a ragged man approached us while we were crossing the great meadow. Mr. Haworth, nervous and excitable, became suspicious and said, "I don't like that chap. He's up to something."

"Oh, nonsense," I replied. "He's only a poor creature anxious for charity."

"I don't know," said he. "I've heard of queer doings in this park."

At that moment the man walked up to us swiftly and said something in a low tone. Instantly Mr. Haworth turned on him in amazing fury and hurled in his teeth the lines of the fiery Tybalt:

> "Alive, in triumph! and Mercutio slain!
> Away to heaven, respective lenity,
> And fire-eyed fury be my conduct now!
> Now, Tybalt, take the 'villain' back again
> That late thou gavest me; for Mercutio's soul
> Is but a little way above our heads,
> Staying for thine to keep him company:
> Either thou, or I, or both, must go with him."

Those words, uttered with the most tragic frenzy and accompanied by a violent gesture, culminating in a furious rush at the astounded man, so terrified him that he ran yelping across the meadow, surely convinced that he had met a lunatic.

"One can't be too careful with that sort of people," said Mr. Haworth. "One never knows what they're up to."

As I learned something of his past, my admiration for Joseph Haworth increased. There was much similarity in the circumstances of our lives. His father was an Englishman from Lancashire; his mother spoke with a strong Lancashire accent. The family had emigrated before Joseph's birth to Cleveland, Ohio, where the elder Haworth secured a position as railway engineer. As the children grew up, they were given jobs at the Cleveland Terminus. But Joseph became enamored of the stage and entered the stock company of the Cleveland Euclid Avenue Opera House. Later he played at the Boston Museum. He supported his widowed mother, helped his brother enter Annapolis, aided his sister and finally purchased a home for the family in Cleveland. All that was done out of his salary of thirty dollars a week, while he himself lived on a strict allowance of seven dollars weekly. Afterwards he was leading man with John McCullough until that tragedian died. He had filled brilliant engagements in New York before acting with me. He was to die at the early age of thirty-five.

Our opening night, December 13, 1887, arrived. This time I was to face a paying, not an invited, audience, and I was surprised to find a fair-sized assembly.

Mr. Haworth had asked if he might have a box for the opening night to invite his friend, Colonel Robert G. Ingersoll,* and

* Colonel Ingersoll (his rank was won in the Civil War) was a lawyer and accomplished lecturer whose publicly expressed disbelief in "the perfect authenticity of the Scriptures," to quote Russell, made his name anathema to many. His agnosticism, which evidently never troubled Julia Marlowe, goes unmentioned in Sothern's text, but the high value to Miss Marlowe's career of his true friendship and scholarly attainments is frequently acknowledged.

his family. I little realized what an important event Colonel Ingersoll's attendance would be for me. He was known to be a great Shakespearean scholar, and I was fortunate so to enlist his interest and sympathy that he became a great help to me in years to come.

I was well aware that the demands made upon an actress by the part of Juliet are far greater than in the role of Parthenia. My success as the latter had been widely heralded, the more so because it had been entirely unexpected. There had been no advance trumpeting, I had appeared, as it were, out of a clear sky. Also the play, *Ingomar,* was regarded as old-fashioned and stagy. The nature and the humanity I had succeeded in lending to my performance accounted for the favorable impression I had made. But here in Juliet was an undertaking of a different kind and of a higher character. The part of Juliet *tests the resources of the most accomplished, the most experienced actress.

Footlights on. Curtain up. I played my best.

After the balcony scene Mr. Ingersoll encountered William Winter, dramatic critic of the New York *Tribune,* in the lobby and asked for comment.

Mr. Winter replied that, though it was much too early to make any comment, my Juliet seemed a sweet and sympathetic girl, but that any young woman would probably do as well under the circumstances. Telling scenes, said Mr. Winter, were yet to come.

Mr. Ingersoll laughingly declared that every act is a test of itself and that I had played the balcony scene magnificently.

* The Sothern manuscript gives no description of Julia Marlowe's appearance when she played Juliet that night. Probably he intended that task be performed by Falk's lovely photograph which speaks more eloquently than words. The portrait is reproduced in the section following page 114 of this volume.

Pronouncements by a Shakespearean authority of Mr. Ingersoll's repute probably diminished the small amount of enthusiasm I had succeeded in planting in Mr. Winter's bosom. Distinguished critics do not relish having their opinions directed by anybody, high or low. However, all's well that ends well; Mr. Winter subsequently became a good friend and supporter of mine.

Romeo and Juliet received approval from our audiences. Mr. Haworth made a fine Romeo, not so much ideal in his appearance as in spirit and execution. Had he lived he would have been recognized as one of the bright geniuses of the American stage. After the killing of Tybalt the audience rose to Joseph Haworth. Men stood up and shouted "Bravo!" and women actually got up on their seats and waved their handkerchiefs. I never have heard such an exhibition of enthusiasm in any theatre. His power was quite overwhelming. Also his solicitude throughout the performance for me and for my success was very touching. At the end he seemed almost as glad as I over what he called my triumph in a difficult part. At the final fall of the curtain he brought his friend, Colonel Ingersoll, and his family to my dressing room to congratulate me on our success. From that time forward the Ingersolls were my staunch friends and supporters. I became almost a member of their household. During my holiday I lived with them at "Wave Crest," Far Rockaway. There I studied Imogen in Shakespeare's *Cymbeline*. One day Mr. Ingersoll remained away from his office to hear me read the part, all his family assembled about him. His comment was, "My child, your mouth was made for Shakespeare."

As I look back on those years, I realize how much strength

I derived from his encouragement. What a privilege I enjoyed in being on such familiar terms with his family! Every day was a new revelation of his wonderful and well-stored mind, his high ideals. The unselfish nobility of his character was revealed constantly in a hundred ways. It was an education for me only to be in his presence, and my mind, long limited by my devotion to one circumscribed object, began to open like a flower under the sun.

From Robert Ingersoll I acquired my first knowledge of the great English poets as distinguished from Shakespeare. He had the happy faculty of not only informing but of exciting a restless eagerness for knowledge. He taught me to love history by conversations at the dinner table, conversation which touched lightly, gaily, learnedly on many topics. He would lead, suggest, provoke, listen with enthusiasm and approval—correct with wisdom and kindness. His interests were widespread: distinguished statesmen, lights of the legal world, important people in literature and art.

To return to my week at the Star Theatre—on the second night, Lester Wallack, the noted actor and manager, came to the performance of *Ingomar*, after considerable persuasion on the part of my management.

Half a century of contact with aspiring ladies had not filled Mr. Wallack with enthusiasm for such evenings away from his cosy fireside, his books and his innumerable friends. He must have exclaimed, "Oh, Lord, another of these stage-struck women! I suppose I'll have to go." He had been of the opinion that it was quite impossible for any young and comparatively inexperienced girl to be worthy of the extraordinary commendation which had been bestowed upon my trial performance of *Ingomar*. But when he read the press on my Juliet, his interest was aroused.

After the first act of *Ingomar* he said to his neighbor in the box, "This girl is very interesting, but a year's training in a stock company would be a great benefit to her."

But after witnessing the later acts, he changed his mind. "I was mistaken," he admitted. "Her quality is unique. The drudgery of stock-company experience would do her great harm."

Next day he sent me the following letter.

> 313 West 34th St., New York.
> Dec. 16, 1887
>
> My dear Miss Marlowe,
>   I had the pleasure of witnessing your performance of "Parthenia" on Tuesday evening and I cannot refrain from expressing to you how pleased and surprised I was.
>   Pleased because the performance was most graceful and charming in every way—surprised because in one so young in the profession it was astonishing to see how very, *very* little there was to find fault with.
>   Pray accept my congratulations and my sincere wish that a long and brilliant career awaits you.
>
> > Faithfully yours,
> > Lester Wallack

Now I had two great champions, Mr. Wallack and Colonel Ingersoll.

We concluded our week's engagement at the Star Theatre with performances of *Twelfth Night*. Though it had been played but two weeks before by Sir Henry Irving and Ellen Terry in the same theatre, it was quite as great a success with both the press and public as *Romeo and Juliet* had been.

Mr. Haworth made a superb Malvolio, as excellent in comedy as in tragedy. Newspaper reviews were most appreciative and my "complacency" found no reason for turning into despondency. My one week's engagement brought managers from out-of-town theatres to see for themselves what I was capable of, and as a result I was booked for six weeks' tour: Chicago, Cincinnati, Louisville and the West. Mr. Haworth was not able to accompany me on account of previous New York engagements. To take his place we engaged Charles Wells, a thoroughly capable actor with much experience in Shakespeare.

The tour provided me with a great deal of pleasant material for my scrap book, but our houses were only moderate. Everywhere the reviewers upheld, encouraged and foretold triumph, but a reputation in Shakespeare's plays is not made overnight. It takes a long and weary journey before the paying public accepts a new Shakespearean star. Many fall by the way and with aching hearts sink back into less arduous roles. Among their number I would not be. I had nailed my colors to the mast, and I would not surrender.

It was when we were playing Louisville that I encountered a detractor of mine also on tour—Henry Dixey—he who, told I was ambitious to play Shakespeare, had remarked dubiously, "With that nose?" Bearing no grudge, I went to see his performance.

There was a comic scene in a barbershop which enabled Mr. Dixey to exhibit his agility and ready wit. That night he intro-

duced something new. A boy came into the shop and asked Mr.
Dixey, playing the proprietor, if he would allow some lithographs to be put in the window.

"Whose lithographs?" Mr. Dixey inquired.

"A very pretty actress," said the boy.

"What's her name?"

"Julia Marlowe."

"Is she beautiful?"

"Look at her," the boy said and unrolled the picture.

Mr. Dixey stared at it as if spellbound. "What does she play?"
he asked.

The boy rattled off our repertoire: "*Ingomar, Romeo and
Juliet, Pygmalion and Galatea, Twelfth Night.*"

"At Macauley's Theatre?" Mr. Dixey pursued.

"She's a wonder!" the boy declared, nodding.

"She's a beauty!" agreed Mr. Dixey. "Yes, you can put it in
the window. And say, here's a dollar. You stand outside there,
point at her and tell everybody to go to the show."

Never was an *amende honorable* more fully and flatteringly
made. Though my nose was upturned, it was no longer so at
Henry Dixey.

One morning Aunt Ada broke bad news to me.

"Well, Julia, I'm awfully sorry but we shall be forced to give
the company their two weeks' notice tonight and return to New
York. The money is gone."

I was not dismayed. In my own estimation I was victorious.
I knew that out of the void would come recognition, if I had
the strength to work and wait.

We played out our two weeks and returned to New York.
Shortly after my arrival there I received a note from William

Gillette who was about to present a play of his own, A *Legal Wreck*, at the Madison Square Theatre. He called on me with Charles Frohman, and they offered me the leading part at a good salary.

"No," I refused. "I will play nothing but Shakespeare and the standard plays."

"But," objected Mr. Frohman, "people don't want them."

"Maybe," said I, "they will want them as I shall play them."

Said Mr. Gillette: "*The Hunchback—Ingomar!* They are unnatural. There is no humanity in them."

"There will be as I will do them."

Mr. Gillette persuaded, Mr. Frohman protested.

"Besides," said I, "I don't look well in modern clothes."

"You look charming in that frock you have on," Mr. Frohman complimented me.

But I had hitched my wagon to a star and shook my head.

Then A. M. Palmer sent for me. He told me that Miss Grace Hawthorne, who was to have appeared in Sardou's *Theodora*, could not come to America. A superb production, costumes and properties which had cost a fortune, were on the management's hands. I was offered the position of star with remuneration beyond my wildest dreams. I read the play and shook my head again. No, the part was not for me. I explained my views to Mr. Palmer.

"The people won't have Shakespeare," said he, "unless the star already has a reputation. For a newcomer it's hopeless."

"Still I'm going to try."

"You will waste your time—your youth. There's no money in it."

"Perhaps I will make enough."

"Then will you accept a position in my stock company," Mr. Palmer asked, "and share the leading business with Mrs. Booth?"

"I should have to obey a stage manager, should I not?"

"Of course."

"I could not do that. I must work out my parts in my own way. I must work out the whole play in my own way."

"I can offer you a fine salary," he tempted.

My answer still was—*No!*

The next day I kept an appointment with Falk, the photographer, who had a studio on Broadway at Twenty-third Street. He was impressed by my poses and had seen my performances at the Star Theatre. Then and there he offered to back me with considerable capital.

Once that generous offer had been made and backing assured, everything else needed fell miraculously into place. Madame Modjeska had just closed her season. Her company was intact, and they were prepared in all my plays. Her manager, Mr. Stinson, was approached and a contract signed for the following season. Mr. Barney was to manage me, with Mr. Stinson the advance man, and Augustus Thomas as business manager. Mr. Falk was to have the sole right to photograph me. The company was a fine one, consisting of people who had played with Madame Modjeska for years.

Out of the blue my chance had come. I had been blessed by finding two "angels" in the theatrical sense: a restaurateur and a photographer. But before I could fully take advantage of my great opportunity I came close to a rendezvous with the Angel of Death.

chapter 6

The Other Angel

We must live in the future and have faith in our cause and in ourselves.

I was patient—I had faith—and for twelve years, from 1888 to 1900, I was content to make a mere living that I might win my goal at last.

My contract with Mr. Falk was for the period of six years. I was to receive a salary of one hundred and fifty dollars a week and twenty per cent of the profits, but when my share materialized, it was small. Out of my salary I paid the hotel bills of Aunt Ada and myself; I also provided for my mother and aided some others. I played a repertoire of heavy parts for eight performances a week and during summer holidays I studied new roles and waited impatiently for the following season.

After the first year of the contract, Colonel Ingersoll persuaded Mr. Falk to allow me fifty dollars a week during my vacation, a concession which greatly aided me to maintain my health, often depleted by my labors. But all this time I was happy, happy in my daily toil and happy in my visions of the future. I had no fears and no regrets. My project was afoot. The future would take care of me.

I went to the highlands of New Jersey to spend the summer months and prepare for my season. However I continued my daily rehearsals with Aunt Ada and repaired to Professor Price three times a week.

With some young people who lived in our boardinghouse I played outdoor games. At "catch ball" I was quite expert and was priding myself one day on my efficiency when the ball thrown by an active boy hit me such a blow on the nose that I was convinced that questionable organ was broken. But after much bloodshed and sympathy it was pronounced uninjured, yet it was scarcely improved. Mr. Dixey might now be able to repeat, "With that nose?"

Hardly had I recovered from that injury when, while bathing on a stormy day, I was thrown down by a huge wave, and my poor face was crushed with such violence into the rough stony beach that my nose was actually "put out of joint." I rushed to the bathing house and saw that my nose was crooked! In terror I twisted it back into shape and heard it make a distinct *click* as it resumed its normal position. "Surely," thought I, "I have a doomed nose. Mr. Dixey must have laid a curse upon it." For many days I was greatly depressed, and considered Pascal's reflection on the nose of Cleopatra: "Had it been shorter, the history of the world would have been changed."

Might not my own fortunes be affected by my misadventure? Would my nose be longer or shorter or stouter or even more uppish than ever? At last it regained its natural proportions; at least I was no worse off than before.

Soon the day of rehearsal with my new company arrived. Four of the most important members had belonged to the cast which had supported Madame Modjeska. The leading man was Charles Barron, an actor from the Boston Museum, capable and kind.

The Modjeska people properly were loyal to her method and to the business which she favored in her various plays and they found, as is frequently the case, some difficulty in assimilating business entirely new as mine was. It was necessary, however, to persuade them to follow my direction, as the movement I had so laboriously arranged illustrated not only my part but the entire play. Some few contretemps occurred, and I fear there was a little resentment at the young girl who dared tell "old stagers" that procedures so long considered sufficient could be improved. So it often is with innovations. Bathtubs, I believe, were once roundly denounced by the physicians.

My repertoire for 1888–1890 consisted of *Twelfth Night*, *Romeo and Juliet*, *The Hunchback*, *Pygmalion and Galatea*, and *As You Like It*. The following season I added *The Belle's Stratagem*, *Much Ado About Nothing*, and a one-act play called *Rogues and Vagabonds* by Malcolm Bell in which I played a young man, a strolling player. Everywhere the press treated me with the greatest consideration, and if approbation could have drawn people to our performances, the theatres would always have been full. Our audiences, too, were most appreciative. Yet during that time Mr. Falk lost about twenty-nine thousand dollars. I am happy to say, that his loss was retrieved and that before my six years' contract expired there was a substantial profit, justifying my backer's courage and enterprise.

In May, 1889, when I was playing in Philadelphia, there began a strange feud with Augustin Daly, dramatist and manager —a feud one-sided and no fault of mine. Its story is told in Charles Belmont Davis's book concerning his brother, Richard Harding Davis.

Clarke Davis,* father of Richard Harding and Charles Bel-

* L. Clarke Davis was managing editor of *The Philadelphia Public Ledger*

mont, was a great champion of mine. He met Mr. Daly on the street one morning and began to sing my praises. Mr. Daly was not impressed and presently said, "I'll bet you a dinner at Delmonico's for as many people as you like that in five years Julia Marlowe will not be heard of."

"I'll take you," said Mr. Davis who then wrote me a letter about the wager,* saying he depended on me to win it for him.

Just as unwittingly I stepped on Augustus Thomas's toes. He gave up his position as business manager of our company. I never knew why until one night in 1916 when he was chairman at a very delightful banquet given to Mr. Sothern and myself by the Civic Forum in New York City. Then long pent-up resentment found vent, and Mr. Thomas confessed that my manager, Mr. Stinson, had been indiscreet enough to ask him to go out and get Miss Marlowe a bottle of stout. "I am not a messenger boy," the indignant Mr. Thomas declared, and thereupon I lost the services of my advance man, who was to become a distinguished playwright. I was sorry, for Mr. Thomas had beguiled many a weary journey by making me a book valued highly. It contained clever sketches of all the

---

and the husband of Rebecca Harding Davis, an author like their two sons: Richard Harding Davis, journalist, novelist, dramatist and war correspondent; Charles Belmont Davis, writer and dramatic critic. The Davis home was a gathering place for stage people.

* Russell amplifies Davis's story of Augustin Daly's persistent feud against Miss Marlowe in interesting detail. A power in the theatre and influential with the press, Daly took every opportunity to disparage Miss Marlowe. When she opened in a play in New York, Daly hastened to stage a rival production of the same drama. He stooped several times to that mean-spirited trick—all because of his resentment of the bet lost to Clarke Davis. Julia Marlowe bore Daly's enmity with unruffled calm, and her productions fared far better than his. The latter part of Daly's brilliant career was shadowed by failures. After his death, the theatre in which he had staged so many hits continued to bear his name. It seemed poetic justice that Julia Marlowe came to play some of her greatest successes at Daly's Theatre.

members of our company, with rhymes which pilloried their oddities and weaknesses.

Happily I made more friends than I lost. A dear one was Walter Brackett of Boston whom Colonel Ingersoll asked to call on me and attend my performances. Mr. Brackett was a painter of fish: strings of trout—trout rising at a fly—salmon jumping from the water. Both he and his wife came to like my work, and I grew to know them well. It reached Mr. Brackett's ears that my obligations were heavy and that I was not making much money; he made some inquiries of Aunt Ada who frankly told him my circumstances. Though he was not well-to-do, the dear old gentleman went among his friends and with them contributed five thousand dollars which they asked me to accept as a loan to be repaid in more prosperous days. I gladly accepted and was relieved of much anxiety. It was not so very long before I was able to return the money. The kindness which prompted that generous deed held a tender place in my heart.

Another trusty friend who came into my life at this time was Frank Colfax, hired as my property man and to play the part of Charles, the wrestler, in *As You Like It*. For thirty-seven years, until the day of his death, he remained my devoted henchman.

Colfax, who had spent his youth in California when the West was wild and woolly, was a husky fellow, proud of his agility. He put up a great fight as Charles, the wrestler, and in his enthusiasm at the first performance nearly killed our Orlando, who found it difficult to assume an air of victory. A Detroit paper thus immortalized this feat:

The wrestling match in *As You Like It*, as produced by Miss Julia Marlowe's meritorious support at Miner's Theatre last evening, had an interesting realism. Frank Colfax played the part of Charles and it looked for a time very much as though he was going to set all Shakespearean tradition and the urgent necessities of the plot at naught by almost literally pulverizing Orlando as he was apparently abundantly able to do. Orlando, however, finally succeeded in averting the alarming menace to the subsequent interest of the play and pulled the professional wrestler over his head to a full length position on the stage, and Charles was borne out amid great applause in the demoralized condition prescribed by many years of precedent and the accepted text of the classic drama.

Some disagreement with the management caused Colfax to leave us at the end of 1891. I sent him a Christmas present, which he said was the only remembrance he received during the lonely winter. Two years later, when I assumed my own management, he returned, and from that time on was always in my company. His duties were various: he played parts, looked after the front of the house sometimes, and was often our stage manager. He rehearsed supers and acted as secretary and general factotum. Once he came to my relief with money he had saved from his small salary, thrusting it gruffly into my hand.

Colfax began to keep a book of maxims after I told him that Colonel Ingersoll had counseled me to read a beautiful poem and to think one unselfish thought every day. Colfax tried to follow that advice, though difficult in the face of the many conflicts he had with supers, stagehands, and baggagemen, some of whom had never heard of Lord Chesterfield. I remember one quite desperate fight he had with a noisy fellow who struck him. Colfax retaliated with a blow which disabled his foe and, regarding him sadly, said, "Kind hearts are more than coronets."

In 1891 I suffered greatly from overwork and much private worry. I felt my strength was giving way, but I could not afford to rest. When I reached Philadelphia I went to live with Mr. and Mrs. Alexander McClure. Mr. McClure was editor of the *Philadelphia Times* and a great friend of Colonel Ingersoll's. Mrs. McClure had called on me at the Bellevue Stratford Hotel and insisted on my staying at their home during my engagement. Had I known what was in store for me, I would not have inflicted myself on these dear people.

On the Friday of the first week I played *Ingomar* I was suffering from such a high fever that I was almost unconscious of what was passing. Next morning the doctor forbade me to act. I had typhoid fever, and for eighteen weeks I endured a violent attack which left me weak and prostrated. I do not know what I should have done had I not been blessed with the devotion of Mr. and Mrs. McClure. Had I been their own child they could not have shown greater care nor showered upon me more affection. I was utterly without resources; my salary was stopped by my managers as soon as my earning capacity was affected. I had no savings on which to rely for my "rainy day." Had this long and devastating illness overtaken me in some hotel, I do not know what would have become of me. I had the advantage of the services of three of Philadelphia's best physicians: Dr. Getchell, Dr. Ashurst and Dr. J. William White.

At one time it was decided that my swollen and distorted face must be lanced, but Dr. White said, "No, such an operation would spoil the girl's face forever. She has to make her living on the stage." So they applied belladonna, the swelling subsided and my face was unmarred. Dear Rosalind! Dear Juliet! I came near to losing you forever.

There came a time in that illness when for weeks I was delirious, though there were moments of semi-consciousness, for I can recall queer, distorted pictures floating about me. Clustered on a crystal chandelier I saw hundreds of little Quakers in their sombre clothes and broad-brimmed hats, bowing and nodding gravely, moving about and coming and going day after day. On two large Oriental vases, Chinese and dragons came alive. They had fearful battles—their eyes shone—blades flashed—the dragons and the men were confused in inextricable contortions. The room was hung with red velvet which so excited my sick brain that I seemed to float in a sea of blood.

I raved in my delirium and excitedly acted the friar's cell scene in *Romeo and Juliet*:

> "O, bid me leap, rather than marry Paris,
> From off the battlements of yonder tower;
> Or walk in thievish ways; or bid me lurk
> Where serpents are; chain me with roaring bears;
> Or shut me nightly in a charnel-house,
> O'er-covered quite with dead men's rattling bones,
> With reeky shanks and yellow chapless skulls,
> Or bid me go into a new-made grave,
> And hide me with a dead man in his shroud;
> Things that to hear them told, have made me tremble;

And I will do it without fear or doubt,
To live an unstain'd wife to my sweet love."

Then I would cry out again and again, repeating, repeating, repeating:

"O, if I wake, shall I not be distraught,
    Environed with all these hideous fears?
    And madly play with my forefathers' joints?
    And pluck the mangled Tybalt from his shroud?
    And in this rage, with some great kinsman's bone,
    As with a club, dash out my desperate brains?
    O, look! methinks I see my cousin's ghost
    Seeking out Romeo that did spit his body
    Upon a rapier's point: stay, Tybalt, stay!
    Romeo, I come! this do I drink to thee."

At last I recovered. During my convalescence my bedroom was filled with flowers from men and women who had watched me play. Many letters of good cheer and happy augury came to give me hope and thankfulness. The expense of my illness, and it was considerable, was assumed by Mr. and Mrs. Mc-Clure. I cannot think of them but with a full heart.

When I regained my strength, I told my hosts that it was necessary for me to go to work. My backer, Mr. Falk, had lost money by the disaster to my season. My manager had obligations to meet. Mr. and Mrs. McClure begged me to allow them to adopt me as their daughter and implored me to leave the stage, to abandon the arduous struggle which had very nearly ended my life.

I could not do it. My heart was engaged in my work, and I

could not give up my independence. My good friends were bitterly disappointed at my determination, but I was convinced that a merely social existence would be irksome to me.

During my illness events had marched on. Laurence Barrett, who was starring with Edwin Booth, had heard of my success in Shakespeare's plays and now sought to become my manager and control my future development. He called on me at the McClures' home and unfolded his plans.

First I was to appear with Booth and Barrett in a repertoire at the Chicago World's Fair, and the following season Mr. Barrett was to launch me as his star with a fine company and equipment. It all sounded very delightful, and as I grew stronger we discussed in correspondence the details of our arrangement.

The terms of the contract he proposed were generous. I was to receive a salary of two hundred dollars a week, my maid's expenses, and a salary for her of twenty-five dollars monthly; in addition I was to have sixty per cent of the net profits. The contract was to run for three years with the prospect of renewal. Mary Anderson's brother Joe would be manager, and Mr. Barrett's daughter Gertrude my companion.

Before I could sign the Barrett contract, my existing obligations must be satisfied. Meanwhile I remained with Mr. and Mrs. McClure who advised me as to each step I should take. Joseph Jefferson came to play in Philadelphia and called on me. He was enthusiastic about the performance of young Wallace Eddinger in *Little Lord Fauntleroy* .

"Is it not the case, Mr. Jefferson, that these precocious children never become very good actors when they grow up?" I asked.

He looked at me with a quizzical eye. "Well, I don't know,"

said he. "I myself was accounted a boy wonder when I was a child." I had not been aware that our Rip Van Winkle had been on the stage as a child.

Richard Mansfield called often and sent me flowers every day during the two weeks of his Philadelphia engagement.

Just as my contract with Mr. Barrett was about to be signed, he fell ill and died suddenly. So vanished an opportunity which I believe would have been greatly to my advantage, for Mr. Barrett's ability as a manager with the highest ideals was universally conceded.

Thus was I thrown back once more on my own energy and my own initiative. I decided to continue under the management of Mr. Falk, but an arrangement was concluded with Aunt Ada * which relieved her of further association with my fortunes. However, she received for some time a compensation from my enterprise.

I gathered my company together as well as I could and, although weak and depleted, arranged a tour and played for ten weeks. Critics noticed that my voice lacked its old strength, but I managed to survive and at the end of the season had a small profit.

* Russell gives details which make this termination of the association with Ada Dow seem less harshly abrupt. "Even while she (Julia Marlowe) had been ill, the Ingersolls and other friends were seeking to better her business relations. She had been now four seasons on the stage, working hard and achieving fame, but receiving for her labors only a salary that was little better than a pittance. The oboe player in Barnum's circus band received more. When she went first with Miss Dow to New York, she had signed a contract that gave into Miss Dow's hands the main control of her business interests. Colonel Ingersoll felt that, while this treaty had been just and necessary, the time had come for her to end it and take charge of her own future. . . . Negotiations were begun with Miss Dow and long continued. In the end an agreement was reached by which Miss Dow accepted weekly payment extending over a period until the value of her interest could be purchased, and Julia Marlowe began for the first time to be in full control of her affairs."

chapter 7

"Hoop-la!" Said Grandmother

Scant though my savings were, I invested them in a trip to England, taking my mother with me. I sorely needed a real rest, and it seemed I would best find it amid the scenes of my early childhood. So back we went to Cumberland to stay with my grandmother on her farm near Threlkeld.

On the train from Liverpool I rushed from side to side of the carriage windows to view the exquisite pictures of hill, dale, and cloudbank, sunshine, rain and mirror lake. At Threlkeld station we were met by my Uncle John with a pony cart drawn by moorland ponies—Galloways. Uncle John was a typical dalesman, tall, broad-shouldered, slightly stooped with age, slow of speech but decisive, calm, his smile slow, his handshake firm. The well remembered village fiddler of my childhood was there, too, a bit the worse for wear but playing *Home, Sweet Home* as sweetly as of yore.

"That be daft Watty," said my uncle. "Just as daft as iver."

Soon we drove up a narrow lane, Uncle John chatting in the thick Cumberland dialect into which my mother fell readily. Grandmother's house was a long, low, gray farm house with latticed windows and a roof of flat gray stones, surrounded by a cluster of barns, pig pens and cow byres. Fenced-in flower gardens flanked the door; flowering plants decked the window sills. And yonder stood my grandmother to welcome us.

"Cush, well as niver! Sarah coom heame at last with her

bonnie bairn. I feard you wad nae git here till the edge of dark."

"It'll rain afore neet it's seah glisky," Uncle John remarked.

My grandmother put her arm around me. "Cush, aa niver expected to see you mair."

My grandfather, seated in the corner of a spacious chimney, echoed, "Aa niver expected oot like this." He lit his black and ancient pipe and stared hard at me.

Oh, the comfort of that Cumberland kitchen! The low ceiling, smoke-darkened, the gnarled oaken beams, the dark cupboards and odd hiding places, the latticed windows with bright curtains, the huge fireplace with an iron bar on which could roast a whole sheep called "hung mutton." There was a long oaken table and chairs, a great clock, an oak settle and a buffet, laden with blue and white china and shining pewter. The kettle sang on the hob. Soon we attacked our evening meal: mutton pie, homemade barley bread and leaven bread of oaten meal, cream and strawberries and sweet cheese.

After talk of America, my grandmother read passages from the Bible. Before bedtime she brewed a port wine negus and at my begging sang in a good, strong voice, "D'ye ken John Peel with his coat so gay, that hunted in Caldbeck once on a day," while all joined in the chorus. A great shaggy sheep dog was let into the room by Uncle John who said he had been "lyin' wi' his nose to the bottom i' the door, yammerin' to hisself whiddum like a patch o' daddergrass." We took our candles and went off to bed. As I opened my window and stood looking at the moon, I thought of this wholesome, carefree life and heard the barn owl cry *Too-whit-tee-whoo*.

The next day we went to church in Caldbeck, to visit the graves of my forebears and to see my birthplace. I met a deaf-

and-dumb fortuneteller; such are regarded as gifted of the gods. On a lovely spring day we saw the ceremony of the Rush Bearing, a charming survival of the time when the earthen floor of a church was thick strewn for warmth's sake with rushes. Children nowadays make wreaths and crosses out of the rushes and place them before the altar. I stood by the wishing gate and wished the wish which must not be spoken or it will not come true. Wandering about Cumberland hills, I grew strong and sure again.

My grandmother had never in her long life been to a theatre. Not only had her religious scruples prevented, but her life was far apart from such amusements. She had, however, been once or twice to Carlisle, and there seen the posters which proclaimed the wonders of Sanger's Circus. When I related my adventures in the theatre, the old lady bridled.

"Oh," said she, "you're one of them circus people then. I hear they are a bad lot."

I protested that circus people are renowned for their circumspect lives and that no person given to devious ways can walk on a tight rope or dare the dangers of the flying trapeze with impunity.

"Oh, that's what you do, is it?" she asked.

"Well, no, Grandmother. I have not yet achieved that distinction."

"Do you say 'Hoop-la!'?" inquired my grandmother. "They tell me all the children say 'Hoop-la!' when they come home from the circus."

"No, Grandmother, I don't say 'Hoop-la' yet. I may someday. One can never tell."

"Well, what do you say then?"

I told her I would show her and stood up and recited Juliet's speech:

> "Gallop apace, you fiery-footed steeds,
> Towards Phoebus' lodging; such a waggoner
> As Phaethon would whip you to the west,
> And bring in cloudy night immediately. . . .
> Come, gentle night, come, loving, black-brow'd night,
> Give me my Romeo; and, when he shall die,
> Take him and cut him out in little stars,
> And he will make the face of heaven so fine,
> That all the world will be in love with night,
> And pay no worship to the garish sun."

"It sounds like the Bible," said my grandmother, who was a great reader of the sacred volume and had therefore absorbed a sense of beauty and rhythm. "It sounds just like the Bible," she repeated.

Then I acted for her Rosalind's scene with Celia when she hears that Orlando is in the Forest and asks: "What shall I do with my doublet and hose?"

"I hope you don't wear breeches," indignantly said my grandmother.

"Well, we don't call them breeches," I equivocated.

"Hoop-la!" said my grandmother, apparently apropos of nothing.

But she seemed to be reconciled, especially as my mother and I appeared to be fairly prosperous, and in spite of being circus people wore our frocks in the daytime.

Shortly we went to London where, for the first time, I saw the performances of Henry Irving and Ellen Terry at the Ly-

ceum Theatre; of course they were a revelation to me who had
traveled about with a few sticks of scenery. With greedy eyes
I watched it all and promised myself such splendid sets someday. Also there grew in my heart a desire to play in London.

Perhaps this is the best time to tell of my next journey to
England, which took place following the theatre season of
1891–92. On that occasion I met Sir Henry Irving and Miss
Terry behind the scenes of the Lyceum. Then I fared forth
to pay a visit to Stratford-on-Avon.

Imagine the emotions of a woman who for some years had
acted Shakespeare's heroines, making her first pilgrimage to his
birthplace! I walked about in a sort of dream. I stayed at the
Red Horse Hotel like a good American on account of Washington Irving. The next day was Market Day and, by the river,
country folk in holiday attire crowded around the sheep and
pigs and cattle in their pens. As soon as I stepped into the street,
I was spotted as a visitor by a boy guide, one of the attractions
of Stratford but unfortunately since discarded. This redheaded
urchin hailed me, "Do you want to know all about Shakespeare?" I was eager for that knowledge and confessed it. Thereupon he took me in charge and proved to be as bright-eyed as
he was bright-headed.

"Go ahead," I begged as we walked toward the birthplace.
"Tell me all about Shakespeare."

At once the small guide launched on a prepared lecture, in-
terlarded with recitations from the plays. Facts and speeches
poured out in breathless style with only now and then a pause
for breath, until my head whirled. Fists clenched from the
mental strain, the lad never looked at me but fixed his eyes on

the horizon or the chimney pots. His torrent of words was ri-
valed but not damned by competitors who followed us shouting
that they could recite Shakespeare's life far better than my boy,
a numskull who didn't know what he was talking about.

My guide tackled Shakespeare's biography with determination, glaring defiance at his tormentors. In a Warwickshire dialect he rattled away: "Shakespeare was a play-actor—'e was
born in Stratford—'is father was a butcher. 'E used to kill calfs
and speak poetry while 'e was a-doin' it. 'E married Anne 'Athaway. She lived at Shottery. 'E went up to Lunnon and become
a play-actor. 'E wrote plays. These are wot 'e wrote."

Here he spouted the titles of Shakespeare's thirty-seven plays,
with occasional gasps for air like a fish out of water. He wound
up in this startling fashion: "*Measure for Measure, Comedy of
Errors, Much Ado About Nothing, Love's Labor Lost, Midsum-
mer Night's Dream, Merchant of Venice, As You Like It,
Romeo and Juliet* and Ellen Terry."

Then he inhaled so deeply I thought he would surely sail
away like a balloon, but he was merely getting ready for a greater
effort and began at a gallop:

> "The quality of mercy is not strained;
> It droppeth as the gentle rain from Heaven
> Upon the place beneath: it is twice blessed;
> It blesseth him that gives and him that takes:
> 'Tis mightiest in the mightiest; . . ."

Next he went through all of Portia's trial scene without a
full stop, his restless eyes glancing from the chimney pots to
his rival reciters and from those ragamuffins back to the chimney pots. He finished with a great smile, as much as to say,

"That's over!" Then he pushed back his hair and went at it again. He recited Hamlet's two soliloquies and the dagger speech from *Macbeth*, and I know he would have continued indefinitely if I had not taken mercy on him by diverting him to Shakespeare's career.

" 'E was a play-actor. 'E wrote plays," my guide rushed on. " 'E went to Lunnon and 'eld 'orses at the play'ouse doors, and 'e 'ad a lot of boys and they 'eld 'orses—and they was called Shakespeare's boys—and 'e made money—and 'e come back 'ere to Stratford and 'e bought a new place, the finest 'ouse in Stratford—and 'e went out on a drinkin' bout with Ben Jonson, who come 'ere to see 'im—and they both got drunk, and Shakespeare went to sleep under a mulberry tree. They got drunk on Sunday and woke up on Monday."

Here at last the boy came to a full stop. It may have been a gap in his memory or thoughts of dinner or of what money I would give him. Or he may have been distracted by the other orators who were now gathered in a group on the other side of the street opposite Shakespeare's birthplace. They were whispering and looking at my boy with evidently evil intentions, maybe with the purpose of waylaying him and robbing him of the fruits of his labor. Anyhow my boy, as we say in the theatre, "dried up." For a fresh start he repeated the distressing statement, " 'E got drunk o' Sunday and died o' Monday. He died o' Sunday and got drunk o' Monday. He was a play-actor and married Anne 'Athaway. 'E got drunk."

Finally with a gulp he regained the thread of his discourse and roared to a climax with the Bard's epitaph:

"Good friend, for Jesus sake forbeare
To digg the dust encloased heare:

Blest be ye man yt spares thes stones,
And curst be he yt moves my bones."

I made him promise to write down that epic lecture and send it to me in London. He kept his word, and in due course it arrived in a badly spelled, all-over-the-place scrawl. It was signed "Your lovin' boy."

chapter 8

Critic's Comeuppance

During the season of 1892–93 an interesting event occurred in Indianapolis. The critic of the *Indianapolis Journal* wrote a review of my productions in which he made the statement that my company was a most inferior one, and that the most important members of the organization had merely said, "My Lord, the carriage waits" in much superior companies.

Here was a body blow indeed! And the injustice of the attack made me indignant.

We had with us several members of Madame Modjeska's company, people of reputation and long experience. In addition we had been fortunate in securing the services of Mrs. John Drew * for *The Love Chase* by Sheridan Knowles. Our salary list was for the times a heavy one, and my management had been generous in outlay in order that I should have the best available support. Indeed the one thing which made me content with the small amount of money I was earning was the knowledge that we had an excellent cast and paid them well.

I felt that I had been trodden upon and, like the worm of the fable, I insisted on turning. I demanded that my manager should take an action against the newspaper.

* Mrs. John Drew, Sr., grandmother of the Barrymores, Lionel, Ethel and Jack.

"Quite hopeless," he declared, blanching at the power of the press.

"It is unjust," said I.

He admitted that it was.

"And false," I insisted.

"Entirely," said he.

"Then they must apologize," I determined and maybe I struck an attitude.

"It will be forgotten tomorrow," he said.

"I shall not forget it," said I.

My friend, Morris Ross, critic and editorial writer of the *Indianapolis News* also begged me to take no steps in the matter. Indeed it was Mr. Ross's emphatic praise of me which had precipitated the trouble, for there was a sort of Capulet and Montague feud between the two local papers, and if one praised an attraction, the other more or less damned it.

"No, no," said Morris Ross. "It is quite useless. Nobody will pay any attention to that review."

But I was not to be appeased. My managers had to give way, and we employed counsel and instituted proceedings. I claimed nominal damages, stating that I demanded only vindication.

Meanwhile my poor company had to await the decision of a jury of the twelve good men and true as to whether we were highly accomplished or unutterably incompetent—a trying ordeal—while the opposing forces prepared for the fray.

I went to dine with Morris Ross at his home where another guest was James Whitcomb Riley, the poet. I sat next to him at dinner, and as he seemed to be mildly sympathetic, I poured out my woes to him. I denounced the offending critic soundly.

I reflected on his intelligence, expressed my views as to his possible origin, indicated his probable destination and in general made it clear that such a fellow had no claim whatever to existence.

"I quite agree with you," drawled Mr. Riley.

"Do you know him?" I asked.

"No," said Mr. Riley. "No, I don't know him, but my sister does. She married him."

The case came into court. I could not appear, but the talent of my players was dwelt upon with eloquence by our counsel. Reviews of distinguished dramatic critics were quoted, and the conduct of the defendant painted in its proper colors. The result was a verdict in my favor, and an apology in open court. I waived the question of damages.

I treat the matter lightly here, but I was deeply chagrined at the time. Not only was my pride hurt, for I was proud to have such capable support, but my business sense assured me that such slander would do damage to my cause. When one boy begins to throw stones, other boys are liable to follow his example, especially if the victim should cry out and take to his heels. I felt it incumbent on me to strike back.

At the close of the season I found myself as usual with very limited resources. Therefore I went to Ozone Park, New York, and paid one hundred and fifty dollars for a cottage for the summer. There I lived on my allowance of fifty dollars a week from Mr. Falk, my mother with me and Mr. Price hard by. Nearly every day I took my vocal lessons, and set about preparing the costumes for *Much Ado About Nothing*. I worked with enthusiasm to make our production worthy of the

play. We had played it the season before, but I was determined
to give it new clothes.

Throughout my career I gave close attention to costumes and
properties, to their authenticity and effect, spending increas-
ingly more on those adjuncts to the art of the theatre as my
means permitted it. Indeed it was a day when realism on the
stage was the vogue and considered well worth the cost.

My friend, Charles L. Davis, an actor-manager, literally paid
the piper. When his production of the melodrama, *Alvin
Jocelyn,* was on the road, he advertised it with a brass band
of forty pieces leading a parade of his company.

Twelve sealskin coats were distributed to his lady actresses
on their arrival in a city. Twelve shining silk hats, twelve frock
coats, twelve pairs of patent leather boots, and twelve pairs of
doeskin gloves were dealt out to the gentlemen members of
his cast. On arrival they paraded with the band, Mr. Davis,
resplendently clad, in the lead. A wide-opened evening waistcoat, which he favored, permitted the exhibition of a huge
diamond stud in his shirt. It had been displayed a week in advance in the window of a select jeweller of the city, along with
a collection of other precious stones the manager owned. The
seal-skinned, high-hatted, kid-gloved, patent-leathered proces-
sion walked to the theatre followed by an open-eyed and wide-
mouthed crowd.

Said an admirer to Mr. Davis one day: "That brass band
must cost you a fortune."

"No," confidentially replied Mr. Davis. "No, not quite. You
see I carry two men, musicians, who play small parts and double
in brass. Those two play the tune. They head the band and
play the tune—see? My advance man picks up the others in

town. We get them on the train and put our uniforms on them. Our man rehearses them so they know what to do. We hand them instruments, our two men who double in brass begin the tune and the others merely shout 'Poomph! Ha! ha! Poomph! ha! ha!' into their instruments. Simple, isn't it? Poomph! ha! ha!"

In *Alvin Jocelyn* Mr. Davis impersonated a farmer, and taking a hint from a fellow player, Denman Thompson, who flourished with the *Old Homestead*, reveled in bucolic atmosphere. He received many encomiums because he washed his real face in real water with real soap; students of the drama grew eloquent over that one touch of nature. In his farmyard were to be seen real pigs and real chickens; one fowl rendered the press agent hysterical by actually laying a real egg. Davis anticipated the production of Pinero's, *The Squire*, presented by the Kendals in London, by projecting the scent of hay across the footlights.

That passion for realism long permeated the theatres of sophisticated London Town. Hansom-cabs drawn by real horses and even four-in-hands appeared upon the stage of the Standard Theatre. Boats were rowed from wing to wing in real water. Such touches had little to do with real acting, but they drew real money.

Not to be outdone, we in New York had real fire engines in a play called *The Still Alarm*; also motor cars and race horses. I myself was the victim of the mania for realism, when my manager insisted on introducing a real fountain with real water into the balcony scene of *Romeo and Juliet*. What Bulwer Lytton describes as the "murmur of low fountains which gush forth i' the midst of roses," it was declared, would enhance the beauty of those tender confessions indulged in by Verona's lovers.

The hateful fountain behaved well enough at rehearsal. But overcome maybe by stage fright or misdirected ambition, it contributed such spasmodic gurglings when poor Juliet began to breathe to the moon her adoration for Romeo that no one but a capable plumber could have controlled its utterances.

"Romeo! Romeo! Wherefore art thou Romeo?" *Phit! Phut! Gurgle! Squirt!* went the water.

"How silver sweet sound lovers' tongues by night." *Tiddle! Babble! Phit!* went the fountain.

"Like sweetest music to attending ears." *Squirt! Gluk-k-k! Fuddle!* gushed the cursed water.

With a final effort to monopolize the attention of the audience, the hose which supplied the water became detached just as wretched Juliet cried: "Parting is such sweet sorrow!" *Phit! Whee-k* went the water and squirted over the whole stage as the curtain came down.

"Never again!" said I.

Since that misadventure managers tried to induce me to encumber my performances with realism, especially Mr. Belasco, who wanted me to play under his management in *As You Like It.*

"We will have real deer," said he, "and real foliage dipping into a real stream."

"No," said I. "I'll stick to real acting, thank you."

In 1893–94 I played in a one-act piece, *Chatterton* by Ernest Lacey, a schoolteacher of Philadelphia. The author was a man of high literary attainments, and his play had great beauty. One-act plays, however, do not attract as much attention in our country as they do elsewhere. I think that is a great pity, for an author may try his wings on such a play, while a manager can afford to risk such a production where he would hesitate at a larger work.

I played the part of the unhappy poet in Mr. Lacey's play with great satisfaction to myself and, I believe, to my audiences.

A curious incident occurred during its first performance in Chicago. The hero dies by poison, powder poured from a small vial. The drug is arsenic, and in order to be quite certain of the effect of the drug and also of the appearance it would have when poured into the glass of water, I consulted my friend, Doctor Ogden, and begged him to explain to me in detail the effects of arsenic poisoning. Doctor Ogden said he would bring to my rooms at my hotel two bottles; one would contain real arsenic and the other sugar of milk powder, which he said was quite harmless, but would look exactly like arsenic. When the powder was placed in the glass it would have the same effect in the water as would arsenic. He brought the two bottles and poured out the arsenic into one tumbler and the sugar in another. They looked exactly alike. He carefully emptied the tumblers and then he handed Teresa, my maid, the bottle of sugar of milk powder and placed the arsenic bottle in his pocket. He explained the symptoms which would indicate that a person had taken arsenic.

I rehearsed carefully the death as Chatterton and then went out to attend to several engagements. At night my maid placed the vial containing the white powder in my pocket, and I went on to play my part. When the moment to take the poison arrived, I poured the powder out and drank off the mixture. I fancied I observed a peculiar taste, and the thought struck me that I had by some error taken the wrong powder. I had to go through my death scene, and as I did so all the symptoms spoken of by the doctor seemed to reproduce themselves most vividly. I sank at last on the bed convinced that I had indeed taken poison. In the play the curtain falls while the lights are changed from night to dawn. When the housekeeper knocks at the locked door and calls out, "Mr. Chatterton! Mr. Chatterton!" there is no answer as the poet lies dead, and again the curtain falls.

As soon as the first curtain fell, I jumped off the bed and cried out frantically, "Teresa, Teresa—you gave me the wrong powder! I am poisoned! I have taken real poison! I am dying! I shall die!"

I heard the applause and the curtain bell and instinctively I fell back on the bed, only to jump up wildly again as soon as the curtain touched the boards and cry again, "Send for Doctor Ogden, I am dying! I have taken real poison!"

Teresa was on the stage, protesting that the powder was not poison, and jumped out of the door just in time for me to take another call. The scene was repeated until I rushed to my room, staggering and moaning with pain and quite sure I was at death's door. Every symptom the doctor had described increased in violence until he came upon the scene to save my life, for I truly believed I was dying.

It was *not* the wrong bottle. I had taken only sugar of milk. But that is an instance of what imagination can do.

From poison to armor was my next step in realism when I decided to produce Shakespeare's *Henry IV, Part II.* I had negotiated with the able actor, William Owen, for the part of

Falstaff, Robert Taber * was to be Hotspur, and I myself had decided to play Prince Hal. I had several reasons for that step. We were in need of novelty. It was necessary to sustain public interest, and we hoped new ventures would provide us with essential réclame. As to the propriety of my appearance as Prince Hal, I argued that since the prince is but sixteen years of age in Shakespeare's play, I might reasonably look the part. I must say, too, the madcap boy had tempted me on account of his delightful qualities, but the question of comporting myself in armor demanded consideration. I determined to take a leaf from Mr. Macready's book. That great tragedian, in order to acquire ease in unaccustomed trappings, used to wear his steel suit at home. He would eat his breakfast and attend to his various duties of the day clad in that cumbersome apparel. It is said that he encountered a tradesman one morning while thus attired. The tradesman regarded the strange apparition for a moment open-mouthed and then exclaimed, "Well, I'll be jiggered!" The tragedian replied severely, "I am not aware, sir, what you mean by declaring that you will be 'jiggered,' but I request that you will cease staring at me and begone!" The man declared that a cat may look at a king, but Mr. Macready explained with such violence what retribution the king would inflict upon any cat who might presume so far that the tradesman fled in dismay.

---

* The capable actor, Robert Taber, had been Madame Modjeska's leading man and first joined Miss Marlowe when she took over members of that company. After co-starring in *The Love Chase* and other plays, they were married in 1894. For a time they were billed as Julia Marlowe Taber and Robert Taber, an unwise decision soon retracted, for managers refused to book Miss Marlowe except under the adopted maiden name she had made notable.

The marriage proved to be unhappy. Julia Marlowe and Robert Taber were divorced in 1900.

I also had some amusing encounters during the summer as I went about in my armor which pinched me here and pinched me there, but I managed to become very much at home in it and especially expert in jumping over a broomstick while practicing an entrance which I proposed to make by vaulting over one of those ancient half-doors which would open into the tavern of Dame Quickly. My figure was slim, and I gradually acquired a manly stride. Falstaff says, "I will sooner have a beard grow in the palm of my hand than he shall get one on his cheek. A barber shall never save sixpense out of it." And again, "Whose chin is not yet fledged." I grew to think I could play Prince Hal.

So I did. It was my colleagues in the play who met with misadventures from arms and armor.

The rehearsals of *Henry IV* proceeded apace, but at the dress one we nearly lost our Falstaff, William Owen. His enormous pad and the piece of armor, the gorget, he wore about his neck caused him considerable suffering in the warm weather, and when he pretended to be dead at the Battle of Shrewsbury, he fell down on his huge protuberance and rolled about like a tortoise.

Prince Hal sees Falstaff apparently defunct and after a very long speech he concludes:

> Death has not struck so fat a deer to-day,
> Though many a dearer in this bloody fray.
> Embowelled will I see thee by and by;
> Till then in blood by noble Percy lie.

The Prince goes off, and Falstaff, rising cautiously, begins a soliloquy:

Embowelled! If thou embowel me to-day, I'll give thee
leave to powder me and eat me, too, to-morrow.

At the dress rehearsal all of us offstage gathered in the wings
to see what our Falstaff would do.

He waited a moment after my exit and rolled on his abdomen
from side to side. He groaned and kicked his legs a bit, his
mailed hands went to his throat. He opened his mouth, gasped
and his face grew contorted.

"Good, isn't he?" said one actor.

"Splendid!" approved another. "So natural."

"By Jove," said a third, "it takes the old school to play a part
like that."

"I think Mr. Owen will make a great Falstaff," I said. We
all turned our regard to Mr. Owen again.

Frank Colfax was holding the prompt book. He popped his
head around the wing and said to me with a look of triumph,
"Isn't he great? I knew he would be."

Mr. Owen was waving his arms wildly. He was now on his
back and he drew up his legs and kicked them out again. His
eyes stuck out of his head, his tongue lolled out of his mouth,
he gasped loudly.

"What a great actor!" an onlooker cried.

"Yes," said another, "and he didn't do any of this at other
rehearsals."

"Oh, but he'd thought it out. This is all thought out."

"Look at that!"

Mr. Owen had seized the foliage drop, which is attached
to a sort of netting, and was trying to lift himself from the
ground by it.

He stared frantically at me, one hand at his neck, and gasped in a strangled voice, "Dying—da—da—" His voice faded into nothingness.

Colfax shouted, "What's he saying?"

"Give him the word!" said somebody.

Colfax rushed to his book. "Embowelled," he prompted in a hoarse whisper. "Embowelled."

"Dying!" the strangling Owen groaned.

"No, no!" shouted Colfax. "Embowelled—if thou embowel me to-day—embowelled. Go on."

I went to Colfax and seized his arm. "He's in trouble," I said.

"I gave him the word, but he won't take it," said Colfax, getting angry.

Two or three actors called out, "He *is* in some sort of trouble."

"Dying!" gurgled Owen, his tongue out. Colfax rushed at him and saw that he actually was strangling. He undid the iron gorget and shouted for help. The armor was stripped off, and Mr. Owen was resuscitated.

"I nearly went that time," said he.

And indeed it was true. The pad had pushed the gorget into his throat when he fell. He had endured during my long speech and then almost suffocated.

Robert Taber, my Hotspur, was the next victim. On our opening night, during the fight between Hotspur and Prince Hal, Mr. Taber's attention was directed to some supers who were engaged in conflict at the back of the scene, and he failed to guard a blow from my huge, two-handed sword. It descended on his head with all the nervous energy of my first performance.

Blood streamed from under his helmet which my stroke had forced down on to his forehead with such force as to wound him quite severely. He staggered and fell, and I, terrified, took off my tabard, which I placed over his face, so that he might not have to show his pain to the audience. I helped him to lie down and asked was he hurt and how badly hurt. "No," said he, "no, go on." But there was much blood and gore, and it was with a fearful heart that I concluded the scene.

Certainly there is such a thing as too great realism on the stage.

chapter 9

An All-Star Cast

While I was grateful to those who had hitherto taken part in the conduct of my business, I felt that I was fully fledged at last and capable of conducting my own affairs. It was, therefore, with a new sense of adventure that in the season of 1894–95 I continued under my own management. My resources were small, but I was armed with confidence and hope, and the constant support of the best critical opinion had given me strength to pursue the path I was persuaded led on to distinction and independence. By extreme economy I had saved enough money to provide a sufficient production for my new adventures. They were *Colombe's Birthday* by Robert Browning and *Henry IV, Part II* which I have already mentioned.

Rehearsals of the former plunged the members of my company into some confusion of mind, for we were no longer dealing with the lucid expression of Shakespeare. The many Browning societies had spread the doctrine that the poet's excellence consisted to considerable degree in the obscurity of his meaning, and it seemed that to interpret him to the best advantage it would be necessary to say one thing and mean another. Indeed to be readily understood would exhibit a distinct inability to comprehend the subtleties of the master. Hence there was some surprise among those who were not already Browningites that in a general way the significance of the lines was evident. "It seems plain enough," one would say in a puzzled way. "I think I get at his meaning." Yet there was a sort of fear that one's intelligence was astray and that one had not dug the incomprehensible out of the commonplace. "I suppose it's devilish deep," said one actor to another. "I suppose so," the other would reply, "or there would be no reason for all these Browning Debating Societies."

My old friend, Thomas Coleman, an excellent actor, played the part of Guibert. He was one of those admirable players who always take great pains to come to the first rehearsal "dead letter perfect." To my surprise he appeared greatly perturbed. He walked about with his hand to his head and every now and then he made gestures of despair. He consulted with other people in corners, and a great shaking of heads ensued.

Tom spoke a line: " 'You hang a beacon out should frogs increase.' "

"What's that?" I asked.

" 'You hang a beacon out should frogs increase,' " repeated Tom.

"No, no," said I. "*Fogs*, not *frogs!*"

"It says 'frogs' here," persisted Tom.

We examined the part. "A mistake of the typewriter," said I.

"Thank heaven!" said Tom. "I could not see what on earth one wanted a beacon for to frighten frogs with. One hears of frogs in people's coats and frogs in people's throats and frogs on railway lines. I thought perhaps there was something subtle about it. But it's a devilish speech anyhow. I have been up all night over this part with a cold towel on my head and black coffee until three in the morning. I'm glad Browning means something after all."

After the play opened, I attended a small reception of learned ladies, one of whom addressed me with many compliments on my performance. I was grateful and flattered until she explained that she saw in my interpretation a thousand profound revelations of the poet's meaning and intention of which I was myself wholly unaware. I thought of those wiseacres who are assured from the text of *Hamlet* that Hamlet is a woman and that Horatio is in love with "her" and that when the dying prince sighs "the rest is silence," he really means "Please don't mention it to anybody." One might push the matter a little further and insist that Horatio should say, "Goodnight, sweet Prin*cess!*" It is only a matter of two letters, a very possible compositor's error.

One should not laugh at learned societies, but I was reminded of the New York ladies who drove to Central Park on Shakespeare's birthday to place a wreath at the base of the poet's statue. An address extolling Shakespeare was read, and a beautiful wreath was propped beside the pedestal, a wreath with a ribbon lettered in gold: "To the immortal author of *Richelieu.*" It was reported later from England that Bulwer Lytton had turned in his grave.

After opening my season on the road I returned to New York and staged *Romeo and Juliet* at Wallack's Theatre. Then I played Miss Hardcastle in *She Stoops to Conquer*, Julia in *The Hunchback*, and Prince Hal in *Henry IV*. In acting the last-mentioned role I finally came to agree with Sarah Bernhardt's conclusion that a woman should only play a man's part when it suggests a man's intelligence in a frail body. That applies to women who have mistakenly, I believe, played Hamlet, a virile and robust character like the historic Prince Hal. My figure

Julia Marlowe as Admiral Sir Joseph Porter in a children's performance of *H.M.S. Pinafore*.

As Rosalind in *As You Like It*. Photograph by Falk.

Photograph by Falk   © Museum of the City of New York

Julia Marlowe as *Juliet*

As Parthenia in *Ingomar*, her first performance in New York. Photograph by Rose & Sands.

E. H. Sothern as Hamlet. Photograph
by Arnold Genthe.

A photograph of the painting by Irving
R. Wiles.

Original watercolor by E. H. Sothern
Switzerland, 1923

Julia dislikes her costume for *Imogen*

Watercolor sketch
by E. H. Sothern, 1923

As Mary Tudor in *When Knighthood Was In Flower*. Photograph by Rose & Sands.

The Sotherns on vacation at San Marco in Venice.

was slim, and I felt I lacked the physical quality. Accordingly I abandoned my expensive production of *Henry IV*, though it made me downcast after so much work and loving care.

A proposal came from the famous Joseph Jefferson for me to make one of the star cast he was organizing to play in *The Rivals*. The engagement was to be for six weeks, with a private car and a diner for the company. The remuneration was good, and considering my financial situation, I was glad to accept the engagement.

The star cast consisted of:

SIR ANTHONY ABSOLUTE	William H. Crane
CAPTAIN ABSOLUTE	Robert Taber
FALKLAND	Joseph Holland
ACRES	Joseph Jefferson
SIR LUCIUS O'TRIGGER	Nat C. Goodwin
FAG	G. M. Holland
DAVID	Francis Wilson
MRS. MALAPROP	Mrs. John Drew
LYDIA LANGUISH	Julia Marlowe
LUCY	Fanny Rice

Performances of *The Rivals* with that cast were a great popular success and drew a great deal of money. Personally I do not much care for star casts. The stars with the best will in the world often overweigh the characters they assume and a well-balanced presentation is hardly possible. But then I imagine such a performance is more what we in America call "a show" than an ordinarily expert performance of a play would be, and people go to see celebrities in a bunch—to get a run for their money. The play for the moment is not at all the thing.

Rehearsals were casual; the call would be to the effect that those could come who wished. There was much amiability and good fellowship and little of that discipline which is most fruitful of results. My habit of precision and much care therefore made me a prey to some anxiety. But the public applauded, and the end was attained.

I had bought a new and correct dress for my character of Lydia Languish, with the sides built out, bustle-wise, as was the fashion of that day.

Mr. Jefferson accosted me on the first night behind the scenes. "Miss Marlowe, Miss Marlowe, what made you get a dress like that?"

"Why, this is the correct costume, Mr. Jefferson."

"Yes, yes, yes—but—those—those things at the sides; they make you look enormous. I wouldn't have them. No—no—I would do away with them."

"But that would ruin the dress. It's absolutely the proper style."

"Nonsense," said Mr. Jefferson, and snapped his fingers in the direction of the audience. "They don't know anything about all that—not a bit of it—nothing, nothing at all. An ounce of effect is worth a pound of correctness," said he.

I wore my dress all the same, for I was of the same opinion still.

A moment later Mr. Jefferson addressed himself to Mr. Taber, playing Captain Absolute. "What's that metal thing you have about your neck, my boy?"

"Why, that's part of my uniform, sir."

"And that stiff collar which seems to choke you and that

white wig. Why you've ruined all your good looks. What do you do that for?"

"But this is the uniform of the time, Mr. Jefferson. I took a lot of trouble to get the exact thing."

"Nonsense," said Mr. Jefferson. "Waste of time and money, too." He closed one eye and tapped Mr. Taber on his chest several times. "They"—a glance toward the audience—"don't know anything about that. Nothing at all. Effect, effect, my boy. That's what you want. Hang the wig. And this thing and the high collar. Off with them."

But Captain Absolute stuck to his uniform. The new fashion for correctness was creeping in.

It took Mr. Jefferson himself and indeed Mrs. Drew, too, a very short time to dress and make up. Mr. Jefferson told me that about three minutes was sufficient for him. He wore very little make-up, indeed his countenance was so mobile and expressive that any addition would have been detrimental. He just put a dab of red on each cheek, and there was Bob Acres.

Nat Goodwin, although not lacking in assurance, found himself disconcerted while acting with Mr. Jefferson, who would not stick to the text but provoked audiences to laughter by grimaces, gestures, drawn-out exclamations and repetitions until poor Mr. Goodwin would be all at sea. He would beg for a rehearsal at which Mr. Jefferson would correctly give the cue saying, "There you are, Nat. That's your cue."

"Yes," Mr. Goodwin would say. "I recognize it, but at night you talk all round that cue and keep the people in an uproar so that I can't fit my lines in anywhere."

Mr. Jefferson would promise amendment, but the unhappy Mr. Goodwin suffered still.

There was an ancient custom of taking calls on the scene while the actors who had not gone off with the victorious character, whose exit was the signal for enthusiasm and applause, were compelled to stand on the stage like so many waxworks. That practice, abhorrent and inartistic, was adhered to by Mr. Jefferson. He and Mrs. Drew also would come on again and again at the door which had just closed on them and bow and bow and bow. I was one of the victims of that deplorable breach of realism and had to wait to go on with my part.

Another custom (now defunct), with its origin in the old-time dimness of the stage lighted with candles, like the first production of *The Rivals*, was the following: Actors would pick up chairs, take them down to the footlights, seat themselves with their faces to the audience and there conduct their conversation so that the full countenance might be observed. That was continued by Mr. Jefferson and Mrs. Drew in spite of modern electric lights. But enough of carping. They were devotedly loved by their public who, as Mr. Jefferson said, "don't know about these things."

On train trips Mr. Jefferson was charming and amusing, a delightful storyteller and an amiable host. He made etchings, printed them on a sort of wringer and presented them to us. He also painted in oils, using a feather in place of a paint brush. His paintings were usually of Louisiana swamps, trees covered with hanging moss. It is altogether a most happy memory to have played and journeyed with that kindly gentleman.

To me Nat Goodwin was a source of perpetual merriment, a born funny man and a wonderful mimic. One day Mr. Jefferson, who had been laughing with the rest of us at Nat Goodwin's imitations, said, "Now, Nat, imitate me."

"Oh, no!" Mr. Goodwin protested. "Oh, no, governor, I couldn't imitate you." But while he spoke, he was giving the most marvelous imitation of Mr. Jefferson, our chief being quite unaware of the fact. The rest of the table was convulsed with laughter as Mr. Jefferson continued to beg for an imitation, and Goodwin in Mr. Jefferson's actual voice avowed he really could not do it. Both men had remarkable countenances with a great variety of expression. Goodwin especially could alter his face to a resemblance of any person he was mimicking. David Garrick's restless mask must have been somewhat similar.

With the money I had been able to save from *The Rivals* I went abroad—to Paris—to Florence—to Venice.

In Paris I went to see Madame Bernhardt play, and she sent for me to visit her behind the scenes. She was standing in the passage which led to her dressing room—she had been playing *Adrienne Lecouvreur*—and the members of her company were gathered about her paying her court, kissing her hand. She embraced me, placed me in a chair, and we chatted as she took off her make-up.

"Why don't you play Adrienne?" she urged me. "You would be charming, charming."

"Oh, Madame," said I. "Madame Modjeska has played that role in America so often I fear I would not be accepted in it."

"Modjeska? Oh, an old woman. She is too old."

At that time the great Sarah was much older than our dear Modjeska who was thus waved into the discard.

Madame Bernhardt was kind and encouraging about my

work and enthusiastic about the high purposes of the theatre. It was a tonic to talk with her.

Encouragement from the Divine Sarah could be coveted by any young actress. But praise from the great Eleanora Duse was still to come my way and that was praise indeed.

chapter 10

Eleanora Duse

At the time I was playing *Romeo and Juliet* in New York, Madame Eleanora Duse was filling an engagement at Miner's Fifth Avenue Theatre. She was giving but four performances a week as was the custom with Italian actors.

Madame Duse attended one of our early performances with a party of friends and several times she stood up in her box, leaned out toward the stage and with arms outstretched she led the applause, looking from the actors to the audience and back again to the actors. Her action was ungenerously misinterpreted as over-demonstrative in one of the newspapers. Americans are a little shy about enthusiasm.

On another occasion to my surprise and pleasure Madame Duse came to see our play. Again she led the applause and sent word that she would like to talk with me after the performance. She had come this time accompanied only by a painter, Signor Gordigiani. When she entered my dressing room, she embraced me and, putting me into the one armchair, she sat on a low trunk holding my hand.

"How young she is," she said to her escort. "How young, and is she not beautiful?" (Really, I must report faithfully.)

She went on to appraise our work with discernment and great generosity. She said that all the business which I had conceived and worked out in the playing of Juliet was practically identical with what she had herself evolved. She had made a great success as Juliet at the age of fourteen in the arena at Verona.

"Gordigiani must paint your portrait," she cried. "He must paint it. He has a studio here at the Carnegie Building. He has painted a beautiful portrait of me." She turned to the artist. "You must paint her at the moment of the kiss."

The painter declared he would be delighted to do so and began with great enthusiasm to explain what the pose and the background would be. All the while Madame Duse was holding my hand and smiling eagerly. I have never seen a sweeter smile. I had heard how remote and secluded she was and how seldom anyone could obtain a glimpse of her, yet to me at this first meeting she was tenderness itself as a woman and generosity itself as an artist.

"Oh, but you must not play more than four times a week," she cried. "To work like this for eight performances a week! It will take ten years off your life."

"For you," said I, "it can be arranged, but not for me. The managers could make no profit by such a plan."

"Oh, it is murder!" Madame Duse exclaimed.

During this time Madame Duse was asked by some friends to play Juliet for a certain charity in New York. The promoters requested me to lend my scenery which I gladly consented to do along with all my properties and furnishings and costumes. But Madame Duse absolutely refused to appear as Juliet and substituted some other role.

"Why should I play Juliet?" she asked. "You have a Juliet. I have sent her some flowers. Julia Marlowe." Again when she was asked the question she refused with, "No, never. Why should I? You have a Juliet good enough for the whole wide world." And for the rest of my season wherever I played there was always a box of flowers at the theatre from Eleanora Duse marked "To Rosalinde"—"To Violetta"—"To Giulietta."

Whenever opportunity offered, Duse and I sought each other out. Once, though she was on tour, I learned to my astonishment that she was in a box in the theatre where I was playing *The Cavalier*. After the play she confessed, "Yes, I ought to be in New Haven, but I am not. I am here." That was one of the peculiarities which troubled her managers and sometimes affected the prosperity of her tours.

"Oh, you must not play such plays," she cried, holding my hand in real distress. "No, no. It is well, but it is not Juliet. You must only play the great roles. I must see you—I must talk with you about D'Annunzio. You must play *Francesca da Rimini*."

She promised to call me on the phone early in the morning, so we could have a talk.

At nine o'clock the phone rang. Could I take breakfast at eleven? . . . Yes. . . . I went to the Savoy Hotel. "You must meet D'Annunzio, act Francesca. No more such plays as that of last night."

I had to explain something which she found it impossible to comprehend. That my American audiences would not accept me in such parts.

"Why?"

"Because," I said, "I can't play the woman with a 'past.' My audiences are accustomed to me in other roles and they will not tolerate me in such parts."

"Oh, the hypocrites," she cried, laughing heartily. "You must leave this country. You must play in Italy. I will arrange

your tour. I will attend to everything. I will lend all my prestige
to the adventure. The Italians and the French must see you
play Juliet. You will be a great success."

The New York *Sun* of January 23, 1903, reported:

A stage box at the Criterion Theatre one evening a week or
so ago seemed untenanted save at the close of each act, when
a woman came to the front, leaned over the rail, impulsively
applauded and threw kisses to Julia Marlowe. It was Eleanora Duse giving public testimony to her admiration and
affection for the gifted American actress.

The friendship between the women began during Duse's
first visit to this country when she prophesied for Miss Marlowe a success she has since won. Duse wondered audibly
why the American has not acted abroad, declaring:

"You would make a furore in Italy and in Germany too
where Shakespeare is understood and better beloved than in
America. Your Juliet would achieve a triumph—and in England. There would be no doubt of your success."

Of course I could not attempt any such doubtful venture as
an Italian season. But Madame Duse was all excitement about
it. She has been pictured as a sad, even a morose woman. But
in all her contact with me she was much alive, her face alert
and ever alight with childlike excitement.

I saw her play in her latter years and felt sad. She was still
the great actress, but her feebleness was pathetic. I sent my
card in to her after the matinée, but the boy came back to say
she could see no one. At that moment Morris Gest, her manager, came to the stage door and asked what I wanted. I told him
I had sent in my card but only as a matter of form. He replied,

"Wait a moment," and disappeared. Shortly he returned and asked me to follow him. He took me to a limousine, and there was Duse. She was pale and greatly fatigued, but she smiled as I held out my hand and drew me into the car. I sank on my knees as she put her arm about me murmuring, "Giulietta, Giulietta," and kissing me tenderly. That was the last I saw of a great actress, a dear woman, a comrade.

On April 21, 1924, I received a letter from Madame Duse's companion. The great actress was dead.

It is said Duse was born in a strolling players' wagon, and that she began to act when she was four years old. I always cherished the memory of her attachment to me and treasured these words as praise from genius: *"La plus parfaite vision de Giulietta que j'ai rencontrée dans ma vie."* *

* The most perfect representation of Juliet I have met in my life.

chapter 11

Teresa and Her Seven Devils

If all the world's a stage, and all the men and women merely players, as Shakespeare declares, one of the most unusual parts was Teresa's. Teresa, an original character if ever there was one, served me as my maid for more than thirty years.

Born in Boston, Teresa * began work at the age of ten as a cashgirl in one of the big stores. She next became a nursemaid in a position where she could live out and have her evenings to herself. She earned extra money as a supernumerary in the theatres and appeared in that capacity during the Boston engagements of Edwin Booth and Sarah Bernhardt. That taste of the stage induced her to join the company of the Kiralfy Brothers as a dancer in *The Black Crook*. She advanced from row to row of the ballet and was becoming expert when she shifted to a circus. In Philadelphia she was riding in the parade, dressed in a costume of Charles the Second's time—a red, velvet riding-habit, gauntlet gloves, a huge hat with many feathers —when her horse, a white one with a false tail, took fright at the noise of a steam roller. It ran away up Broad Street and far into the suburbs. A man seized the horse by its tail and to

* "Teresa" is not identified by Mr. Sothern, perhaps because his manuscript, written while she was still living, features so many of her amusing eccentricities. Friends of the Sotherns state definitely that her name was Mary Daly. Their identification is confirmed by a report for 1914–15 of the Dental Department of the American Ambulance, Paris (see end of this chapter), which shows Dr. George B. Hayes as Chief Dental Surgeon and a Miss Daly as Head Nurse during that period.

his amazement the tail came off and the horse went on. Finally the red-habited equestrienne landed in the backyard of a small private house. Its only occupant, a chap suffering from too much good fellowship, heard the disturbance, put his head out at the window and beheld the apparition of Teresa. He screamed for help. Neighbors ran to his assistance, and the lady of Charles the Second's court was helped up and sent back to the circus grounds in a cab, with the white steed tied behind it.

Teresa returned to Boston and took a job as super in my company playing at the Hollis Street Theatre. My maid, having found the work too exacting, had left, and I had enlisted one of the extra women in haste; she, too, was dissatisfied. Consequently she confided in Teresa that I was in need of assistance, and one evening I found a large Irish woman in my dressing room. The super introduced her.

"This girl has had a lot of theatre experience," she said.

"What experience?" I inquired.

"A horse ran away with her," said the super.

"That does not seem to be an experience which will be useful to me," said I.

"She has been with Kiralfy," the sponsor added, "and she can stand on the tips of her toes for five minutes at a time."

"I can't see that that is an accomplishment which will be to my advantage," I replied.

"She's been a cashgirl and made bustles," pleaded the sponsor.

"I don't wear bustles," said I, growing impatient.

"I want to dress you," begged the Irish girl, "and I'll do my best to please you."

I had to have somebody and have her that moment, so I said, "All right, come on." Thus our association of many years began.

The morning after fate bestowed Teresa upon me we left for Chicago. Teresa had been hired at twenty-five dollars a month and her board. In Chicago she appeared at my room at ten o'clock having been requested to be there at nine thirty. She was clad in a purple velvet frock which I learned later she had purchased out of her savings for my special benefit.

I was in bed. Teresa sat down in my armchair, nodded to me kindly and remarked that it was an agreeable day. She appeared in no hurry to assume her duties.

"Will you please get my bath ready?" I asked when I thought the social amenities had been accomplished.

Teresa looked surprised and sat for a moment with her mouth open. "Suppose I will," said she, and as if in doubt about something went into the bathroom, turned on the water, broke a tumbler and, in picking it up, hit her head against the basin. She called out, "Drat the thing," and returned to me holding her hand to her forehead.

"Will you please close the door, Teresa," said I.

"I suppose so," said Teresa and banged it.

"Quietly please, Teresa," I begged.

"I guess you're nervous," said Teresa, seating herself again in my armchair.

"I'm afraid I am," I admitted, "and I'm ill."

I picked up my book. "Will you please call the waiter and tell him to get me some coffee, and in half an hour to bring me an omelette and some dry toast and some more coffee?"

Teresa went to the telephone and knocked several books off

the table. She picked them up with one hand while she held the telephone in the other, dropping the books again.

"I guess I'm clumsy," said Teresa.

That possibility had occurred to me. I did not want to be discouraging, so I said, "Oh, accidents will happen."

"I guess so," said Teresa.

The waiter arrived. "Write the order down," I directed.

As my maid wrote, the waiter looked at her as if he had never seen her like before.

"I hate *him*," she said as the man disappeared.

I had hoped that Teresa would perhaps tidy my room and arrange my garments, but she sat listlessly in the armchair and stared at me. I was reading *Dombey and Son*.

After a pause and some fingering of the purple velvet dress, Teresa said, "I like you."

"I am glad to hear it, Teresa," said I. "That will make your service the more agreeable."

"Aren't you going to read to me?" asked Teresa.

Such was not my intention, but I had a feeling that I must not break Teresa's heart by too immediate discipline, so I said, "Yes, if you like," and I read a few pages.

Teresa yawned without placing her hand before her mouth, and as I put down the book preparatory to getting out of bed, she said, "Say, that makes me tired."

"Indeed? I am sorry," said I, reflecting that Teresa at least possessed the excellent quality of candor. "I am going to get up, Teresa," I announced.

"Go ahead," said Teresa.

"Please give me my bath," said I.

"*Give* it you?" she inquired with immense surprise.

"Yes, please. Assist me in and out of it. I might slip. You can put a towel in front of your dress," for she was looking down at the purple velvet with some concern.

The bathing episode passed in silence. After I had dressed, the waiter brought my tray. It contained cold ham, not an omelette.

"Why didn't you order an omelette?"

"I couldn't spell it," said Teresa, "but I knew how to spell ham."

The possibilities of my future diet rather appalled me, and I began to wonder how many dishes Teresa might be capable of spelling. However I phoned for my omelette and was silent.

"Say, I like you," again said Teresa.

Once more I answered that I was gratified and added that it was always a pleasant thing for a servant to be pleased with her mistress.

"Servant!" ejaculated Teresa.

"I said 'servant,'" I repeated. "That, Teresa, will be your position if you choose to remain with me."

"I guess I'll stay," Teresa replied.

"Now," said I, "you may go about your duty and please hand me that box of gingerbread." I took a piece and offered her some.

Teresa took a piece, drew up a chair and sat down at the breakfast table.

"You may take the gingerbread into the sitting room, Teresa, if you wish to eat it," said I. "Then you may get my clothes in order, clean the room and go to the theatre for my mail."

Teresa threw the gingerbread on the mantelpiece and flounced out of the room.

Meanwhile Miss Olea Bull, daughter of the great violinist and member of my company, called to see if she could be of any service. At once she perceived the disorder of the room and began to straighten it.

Teresa reappeared and, seeing the pretty lady performing her duties, said with a bad grace, "Say, I'll do that."

"Oh, no, not at all. I love to help Miss Marlowe," said Olea. "Indeed, Teresa, my mother is here visiting me, and she is going to come up every day and prepare food for Miss Marlowe. We are going to see that she has good things to eat. My mother is a famous cook and a great housekeeper. We are going to get Miss Marlowe well and see that she has every possible attention."

Teresa seemed to be engaged in an inward struggle. Her demons were at war within her. At last she seized a towel from Olea's busy hand and went to work. For a day or so she attended to her job with a certain solemnity but she attended to it.

Meanwhile I tried to instruct her. "When people call, Teresa," I asked, "please answer their questions simply and politely but do not enter into conversation. They do not expect you to smile or to laugh at them. I think that quiet dignity, which suits you so well, is the best manner to assume."

"Mayn't I laugh?" said Teresa.

"By all means," I conceded, "but people will not expect you to laugh at them when they are calling on me. Now I am going to lie down and I am not at home to anyone."

Mrs. Ole Bull called shortly. Teresa went to the door, and I heard her say, "She says she is not at home."

"Oh, does she?" said Mrs. Bull. "Well that means that I can

come in." Come in she did and began at once to nurse me and cook and generally take charge.

For two weeks she cared for me as though she were my mother. She nursed me back to health and put me on my feet once more.

"Say!" said Teresa to her one day, pointing at a photograph which Mrs. Bull had given me. "Say, who's that?"

"That," said Mrs. Bull, "is my husband."

"He's holding a fiddle!" observed Teresa. "What's he do for a living?"

Mrs. Bull put her finger to her lips and whispered, "He plays the violin but don't tell anybody."

Frank Colfax, my stage manager, came to see me one day, sat by my bed, told me the news and read from his little book of maxims.

"You're looking well, Teresa," he told my maid.

Teresa who had at my suggestion discarded her purple velvet and now wore a print frock I had provided for her, snapped, "What's that to you?"

"I hope you're taking good care of Miss Marlowe," I heard Frank say.

"None of your business," Teresa retorted.

"Well," said Colfax with a fine sarcasm, "I hope you're fond of yourself, for nobody else is."

"You keep to your stage work and don't come nosing in here. I'm a lady," said Teresa.

Said Frank, "You're a sophisticated rhetorician, inebriated with the exuberance of your own verbosity, and gifted with an egotistical imagination which can at all times command an interminable and inconsistent series of arguments to malign an opponent and to glorify yourself."

"Frank!" I cried out to him. "What on earth are you saying to her? Where did you get the rigmarole from?"

"It ain't riggermarole," denied Frank, his eyes flashing. "It ain't riggermarole—it's Disraeli."

Teresa's progress in the amenities was slow, for I calculated that she was possessed of, at the very least, seven devils. Their antics were unexpected and alarming. She would be sullen or violent or tearful, according to the particular fiend which happened to control her. Her contrition was pitiful, but her tantrums were not convenient.

But I am a creature of habit and I had acquired the Teresa habit. I felt that she was after a fashion devoted to me, attached as a barnacle is to a ship. I would have to go into dry dock to get rid of her. She had no qualifications whatever for a lady's maid. She was untidy, negligent, disobedient, noisy, forgetful, ill-humored and a slattern about her own person. She could not write a note without upsetting the ink. She could not shut the door without slamming it. She insisted on talking all the time about everything and about nothing. She either loved or loathed the people who came in contact with me and did not hesitate either to tell them so or to indicate her inclination or her aversion by eloquent pantomime. But her occasional, "Say, I like you" did gradually have its effect. I suppose we are all subject to the melting influence of such flattery.

Occasionally Teresa's seven devils would seize her in the middle of a performance and she would, over some small matter of haste or impatience on my part, rush from the dressing room and leave me half clad, either to struggle with my own finery or to cry out for help.

Once or twice she went away for several hours at a time, leaving ill-written farewell letters, tearful and resentful, but she returned and was forgiven. Once she had remained away a day and a night and met with awful adventures. First she was robbed of all her money. Next she was burned on the forehead by an eccentric fellow who had accosted her and when she resented his attentions, branded her with his glowing cigar.

I had scoured the city for her and when I returned, worn out, to my hotel and cried to my friends, "Where can she be?" a thin voice from behind a window curtain whined, "I'm here" and a bedraggled Teresa—wet through, hollow-eyed, repentant —fell on her knees.

Harum-scarum truant chasing was no pastime for a hard-worked person like me. I denounced Teresa and threatened that the next time she bothered me she must go.

"Say, I like you," Teresa murmured.

One day I made an arrangement in a hotel for her to take her meals in the servants' hall. On one occasion she came up from her dinner and demanded, "I want more wages! And if I don't get it, I go!"

"I have no more money to give you, Teresa," I replied, and it was quite true, for my resources were stretched to the limit. Teresa announced with a sniff, "Lillian Russell makes seven hundred and fifty dollars a week and she has a suite of rooms, and *her* maid has a fine room with a bath and fifty dollars a month. And she carries her own cook."

"Miss Russell, I am sure, deserves her good fortune. But I have not yet achieved it."

"The Leffingwell's valet gets two hundred dollars a month, and his boss allows him to treat all the other servants to champagne. We just had champagne for dinner. His boss pays for it."

"Did these people tell you to ask for more money?"

"Yes, and they said if I did not get it, I was to go. They said my honor demanded it."

At last I said, "Well, Teresa, you must be careful of your honor, but I can't give you what I haven't got."

"Then I'm going," was her ultimatum.

She went to Lillian Russell's maid and boasted of her rebellion. Miss Russell had no place for her. She then went to an employment agency, but had to confess she could not cook, wait at table, nor sew, manicure nor dress hair. She spent some of her money on a ticket to New York but found no job there. She slept in railway stations or on park benches, and she did not eat for two days.

I sought her everywhere, and Colfax traced her to a cheap New York lodginghouse. She was feeble from lack of food and weakly weeping.

"Don't you know better than to do a thing like this?" he scolded.

"You shut up!" replied Teresa.

"Get up and come and have something to eat," said Colfax.

Teresa could summon no word of thanks from the mouths of her seven devils. When she was restored to me, she told me her wages would do and admitted she could not find another place.

Once more she ran away, but she telegraphed me where she was. I wired back for her to stay there, as I had done with her.

As I was about to board a steamship for France, there on the deck was Teresa.

"I can't take you back, Teresa," said I.

"I don't want any money," she said.

"I have barely enough for my own expenses, Teresa."

"I don't care about money. I wish I could go with you."

The whistle blew for sailing time. I walked up the gang-plank.

Teresa followed me.

Now comes the most extraordinary part of the saga of the temperamental Teresa.

While I was playing in *For Bonnie Prince Charlie* in New York, Teresa announced one evening in my dressing room that she would like "to go and get educated."

"I'll help you get an education," I offered, "but it means work—long hours of study. It will take you four years to get through college. You'll have to work much harder than you do now."

"Those massage women you have make a good living," Teresa said. "So did the nurses you had when you were sick. They're educated."

"Would you like to be a nurse?" I asked.

"Yes, I would," Teresa responded.

"Good. I'll see my friend, Mrs. Campbell, tomorrow and ask her to make arrangements with Doctor Nuff."

"Tomorrow?" gasped Teresa.

"The sooner you start the better."

"But I don't want to leave you."

"You can't eat your cake and have it, too. If you really want an education you must give up my service and go out and work for it."

My friend took Teresa to the City Hospital where Doctor Nuff was head physician. Teresa was admitted to probation for two months. Every other day the probationary nurses had to attend "Dictation." Teresa, fearful of her weakness in spelling, missed the first two lectures purposely. Her attention was called to the delinquency, and the superintendent said, "I shall want you to tell me what you know about burns."

"Oh, I know a lot about Burns," Teresa boasted.

"What for instance?" asked the superintendent, surprised.

Teresa recited fluently:

" 'Wee stickit, cowerin' timorous beastie,
    O what a panic's in thy breastie.' "

"No, no," laughed the superintendent. "I mean when people are burned—suffer from fire. I'm afraid the poets won't serve for plasters."

Teresa went to dictation. Her paper was covered with so many blots and smudges that the superintendent cried, "Why, this is awful! Why, here's one word spelled in eight different ways."

"I'm not narrow-minded about spelling," said Teresa. "And besides spelling never cured anybody, did it?"

"Well, no," the superintendent admitted.

Teresa was allowed to continue her courses and starred in arithmetic. Finally she passed her examinations with flying colors, being either third or fourth in every subject out of a large class.

She worked for three years, receiving nine dollars a month

and her board. She was about to be examined for her diploma when she fell ill and was suspected of being consumptive. I sent her to my house at Highmount in the Catskills, where she stayed three months and gained thirty pounds. Her cure astonished the doctors. She was admitted again to the hospital and obtained her diploma as a full-fledged nurse.

Shortly she went to Portland, Oregon, and found employment in a home for the aged. There still were few dull moments when Teresa was around. One evening when the ancient inmates were gathered together for mutual entertainment, Teresa dashed into the room, clad in an improvised ballet costume with flowers in her hair. Thereupon she performed a hornpipe and a *pas seul*, worthy of her *Black Crook* days. She was invited to resign the next day.

When she again asked my help, I told her I would give her the freedom of my little flat in Paris and an allowance of five hundred dollars a year so that she might study. She was to find a teacher who would instruct her in various subjects and tame her seven devils. When I wrote and asked her how she liked her life, Teresa replied, "My life will be the death of me."

When the First World War began, Teresa volunteered at the American Ambulance Hospital in Neuilly where she served as an anesthetist. Her seven devils banished, she became a ministering angel to hundreds of wounded men, caring chiefly for those with dreadful facial wounds. She exhibited qualities she never suspected were hers and rose to the position of head nurse. From the Dental Department she won this citation:

The early appointment of a head nurse was a most useful and necessary expedient for the training and direction of the

Auxiliaries; in the supervision of dressings, the management of the wounded, and for general order. The Department was fortunate in the selection for this post and owes much to the ability and tact with which these duties were performed.

George B. Hayes, the chief surgeon, presented Teresa with a gold medal inscribed: "In recognition of faithful service 1914–1915. Ambulance Americaine, Lycée Pasteur, Neuilly-sur-Seine."

At the end of 1915, Teresa, ill and exhausted, came back to me, back to my warmest welcome.

chapter 12

Ordeal in Tartans

Finding new plays was never an easy task for me. Those I chose must draw public attention to my repertoire and at the same time be of sufficient dignity and merit to be at least to some extent in the Shakespeare category.

Elwyn Barron, a Chicago newspaper critic, had written a play based on George Eliot's *Romola* whose theme and medieval atmosphere attracted me. After visiting Florence and Venice to absorb information and local color, I produced the play with great care, but the public did not respond with enthusiasm, and it was given only occasional performances.

My other venture for the season of 1896–97 was a play called *Les Jacobites* by François Coppée, which had been adapted by J. I. C. Clarke of the New York *Herald*. It was a gloomy but powerful play. The character of Mary, a poor Scots lassie who gives her life for the Pretender's cause, was a part which gave me many fine opportunities. Here I attempted for the first time an entirely tragic role. The circumstances of the drama made it necessary for the heroine to exhibit through the entire story great emotional stress.

There was one scene in *For Bonnie Prince Charlie*, as we retitled the play, where for thirty minutes I had to weep constantly and I studied to do this with great variety. The scene was a tragic and pitiful one in the highest degree.

Before planning the production, I traveled to Scotland to

visit the scene of my play. I drove through the Trossachs on a misty morning, seated beside the red-coated driver of a four-horse team. I explored Rob Roy's dripping cave. In my imagination, always active on such an adventure, I lived the story of the Lady of the Lake. I made raids with the cattle thieves and fought in Border wars. I was at the battle of Preston Pans and saw the faithful Highlanders throw away their feathered bonnets and their plaids and, naked to the waist, dash in with target and claymore, yelling their war cries as they rushed the English guns. At Holyrood I trod a measure at the great ball. I stood by the Tolbooth and watched the Prince go by, and I lifted up my voice and sang with a will, "Charlie is my darling." I mourned at the fatal field of Culloden where the green grass grew red with Scottish blood.

What devotion, love and sacrifice for an ideal, and how sadly was the ideal embodied by the unhappy prince! Think of those seven men of Glen Morriston, who lived like hunted beasts in a cavern high above the glen. One day the ragged, footsore prince stood at the opening of their den, a price of twenty-five thousand pounds on his head. Those men were bandits, cattle thieves, men of plunder and of blood, but for weeks they sheltered Charles. From their eyrie they could see the Duke of Cumberland's troopers in the glen searching for their guest. His worn-out shoes and his ragged clothes were taken away one night as he slept, and he awoke to find clean linen, new brogues, new kilt and coat and plaid by his bed of grass and fir. The men of Glen Morriston had waylaid travelers in the night and replenished their prince's wardrobe.

The leader of the seven disappeared and was absent for many days. At length he stood again in the cavern, his head bound with a bloody cloth, one arm disabled, his feet bleeding and wounded. He knelt before Prince Charlie and from his breast took a small package and fell unconscious. The packet contained some gingerbread, brought through many miles and dangers from Edinburgh for his Liege. Had he been taken, he would, as a cattle thief, have been hanged in chains. From this eagle's nest among the crags Charles saw the Duke of Cumberland's men seeking him high and low, but the seven men of Glen Morriston kept him safe, taking turns night and day for many weeks to keep watch, never tempted by the great reward to betray him.

At last Prince Charlie ventured forth and would surely have been taken had not Flora Macdonald disguised him in women's clothes and guided him to the north through devious ways. A diversion in his favor was made by a young Highlander who resembled the Prince. He donned the royal tartan and faced a searching party. In the fight that ensued, he was shot but before he fell he lifted his claymore aloft and shouted, "Villains, you have slain your prince!" His body was taken to London as that of the veritable Charles, and the search was abandoned. With Flora Macdonald, Charles reached Arisaig and took ship for France.

Our play portrayed that extreme devotion—Oh, the pity of it!—to an unworthy Prince. But Charlie is still a figure of romance who lives in song and story and in the hearts of many Scots to this day. I encountered that living loyalty when I went to Arisaig and looked for someone to lead me to the secluded cave where Prince Charles hid for many days and nights, fed by his country folk until he dared embark.

No English was spoken there—the rough Highland people

knew only Gaelic. Looking for a guide, I saw an old man of about eighty seated in the rain, a bonnet on his white hair and a thick plaid wrapped about his body. Some women were at their work, as I opened a gate and walked up the path. They could not understand a word I uttered. I kept on saying "cave" and "Prince Charlie." The old man was deaf and looked at me through shaggy brows as he puffed a pipe. Finally one of the younger women understood and spoke loudly to the old man. He jumped up, motioned me to follow and almost ran down the path. I clambered up with much difficulty and, there sure enough was the cave. Then I crawled through its small entrance to find a space where one could scarcely lie down with comfort. After letting my fancy picture the bedraggled, hunted man, wretched hero of a lost cause, I climbed down the rocks in the drizzling mist, approached the old man and tried to thank him. I took some silver from my purse and offered it to him. He drew himself up, looked at me with scorn, turned his back and returned to his cottage. I watched him with regret that I had hurt his devotion and wondered that loyalty should flame still in his ancient breast. Culloden was fought in 1745. That old man's grandfather might have battled for Prince Charlie.

Our production had been carefully prepared. Hamilton Bell designed the costumes; * Edward Howard composed the

* The tartans worn in *For Bonnie Prince Charlie* are an example of Julia Marlowe's remarkable attention to detail. Russell's biography relates that Bell, the costume designer, reported difficulty in finding historically correct plaids and advised that material as nearly right as possible be obtained, with any slight inaccuracies explained in a program note. By no means, Miss Marlowe ruled. Tartans must be absolutely authentic. At last Royal Stuart tartan was found— twelve yards for each warrior—and Prince Charlie's personal tartan was woven to order at considerable expense.

music. We carried our own pipers, and the skirl of the pipes
in war or in sorrow through the scenes of the play created a
telling effect. When, for instance, the pibrochs signaled that
the clans had risen and were marching for Charlie, it was extremely stirring.

During that entire scene there were no lines for Mary, once
she had persuaded Lady Clanmorris to leave the room. The
accusations, the denunciations, the tearing from her forehead
of the emblem of maidenhood, the curse of the grandfather
—to all of them she could make no defense, no reply but her
tears. To graduate the shame, the grief, and reach through a
long half hour a gradual crescendo—that was no easy task. I
had the scene read to me a hundred times, while I, alone in
the silent theatre except for a friend holding the book, would
go through all the listening, all the weeping, sobbing, and praying of the wretched Mary. There I profited by my study of the
acting of Clara Morris. The scene was certainly one of the
most interesting I ever attempted.

When the play opened in New York at Wallack's Theatre,
we were encouraged by great audiences. The "standing room
only" sign was out for the first week. Opinions of the press
were generous to a degree, although all admitted the deep
shadow of the story was stressed.

But the second week the attendance fell away. People could
not tolerate so terrible a strain upon their emotions. Many
wrote that they had been uplifted by the exquisite sacrifice of
the heroine. Frequently when the final curtain fell, the audience would remain seated for a considerable time before they
began to leave the theatre, so deeply were they affected by the
play.

For Bonnie Prince Charlie was too much for the average theatregoer. Tragedy and sentiment can be too profoundly, too overwhelmingly presented.

We were playing in a "one-night stand" during this season. I heard a man knock at a door of a hotel room near mine after the play. "Will," he cried, "Will! For the Lord's sake get up and give me a drink. I've just seen a play in which everybody's killed except an old man and he's blind! He's the only one left on the links! For Heaven's sake give me a drink."

This letter from H. W. Williams, a distinguished dramatic critic of New Orleans, will give some intimation of the effect of the play upon sensitive natures:

My dear friend,

I want to thank you for the hours of keenest delight I have experienced in witnessing your exquisite impersonation of Mary. I am glad for my own sake (though not for yours) that I did not have an opportunity of writing the criticism— glad because I felt that anything I could write would be so miserably inadequate. I do not know what Mary would be in any other hands, but in yours she seems a supernatural, a Heavenly, an angel ideal materialized and clothed with humanity. Weak and sinful man that I am and calloused by contact with many who may be worse than myself, I seemed to breathe a pure air and feel the benediction of such a presence as Mary's—such noble, lofty aspirations—such crystalline purity of motive—such grand love of country soaring above the young maiden's first and only human love (which is left like a wounded white dove to beat its tender life out with vain flutterings against Fate's prison bars) cannot but make our lives and our surroundings seem pretty selfish and sordid, and lead us to higher, broader and purer aspirations.

To be perfectly honest with you, I am something at a loss to know how much my enjoyment of *For Bonnie Prince Charlie* may be due to the author, although I well know the lion's share of my thanks belongs to you. In fact the accoustics of the Charles Theatre are so bad that from where I sat last night and tonight I missed much of the dialogue, although I was able to hear *you* pretty well. Indeed I never saw a character which seemed to have so little need of words as your Mary does. When she first appears leading her blind grandfather lovingly and tenderly, when she appeals beseechingly to the clansmen, when she mournfully and tenderly trails upon the ground the flag of Scotland that is to be buried and when she proudly bears it aloft a few moments later, there is no need of words.

What need of words for Mary when with perceptibly blanching cheek and glazing eye she hears the appointment made for the fatal rendezvous, while she feels her warm, loving heart grow cold in her bosom? What words could tell one tenth the anguish that do those sobs, moans and inarticulate cries, that woe-stricken but beautiful face, those frantic but graceful gestures pregnant with a force of lightning-like intensity which speak the theme which is the mainspring of the play in the third act? Even while she sleeps with her glorious face and form wrapped in the blind beggar's plaid, Mary is eloquent in picturesque, softened outline.

My very dear friend, pardon me for boring you with such a long letter. I only meant to thank you for the keen enjoyment your Mary had afforded me—and I hope the good influence will lift me for a time, at least, out of my sordid, every day surroundings.

Always your friend,
H. W. Williams

My repertoire still drew fair houses, but the profit on the season was small, and at the end of the year I had a meager eleven hundred dollars which I could call my own. On that I must spend my holiday, secure a new play and provide costumes and scenery. Surely I needed Fortunatus's cap, the wand of Cinderella's godmother, the assistance of Hermann the Great, and the assurance of P. T. Barnum.

chapter 13

"Too Dear for My Possessing"

Having told Teresa's story, I turn back to earlier in my career and hers in my service.

In preparation for the season of 1897–98, I rehearsed my repertoire in New York with a view to going on the road and opening in Milwaukee. After my tour, I planned to produce a German play, *The Countess Valeska*. It was free from all charges. I had a translation made and worked on the manuscript to fit it for our stage.

In these days I lived practically from hand to mouth, every penny I managed to save one year going into preparations for the next—for costumes and for the inexpensive holidays I needed for rest and recuperation. The day before our start for Milwaukee Frank Colfax remarked that we had better buy the railway tickets for the journey.

I went to my trunk and took out the bag which served me as a national bank. "Teresa," I called, "we haven't any money."

"No," she said. "I paid the hotel bill today and that's all we have."

"How awful!" I exclaimed. "What shall I do?"

Frank took up his hat and left the room.

I knew no one to whom I could or would apply. With all my ups and downs I had never found myself in this predicament before. The possibility of having to close my season before I had begun filled me with dismay. In my despair I sat down, elbows on the table and hands clutching my hair.

At that moment Frank Colfax returned. He took my right hand from my head, thrust something into it and hurriedly left the room again.

I looked at my hand. It held a roll of bills. I could not see. I handed them to Teresa. She counted them greedily.

"Five hundred dollars," she announced. "Where did he get it?"

"I suppose it is all that he has in the world," I guessed.

"Say, I like him!" Teresa said.

So we reached Milwaukee after all and started our season. I met Frank at the railway station but I could not speak to him —I could only take his hand.

For the next few weeks I worked hard, playing at night and rehearsing *The Countess Valeska* by day. Our business was fair, but the strain was great.

I had but one manuscript of my new play, which contained all my carefully prepared business carefully written in. We had played at Jamestown, New York, and early the next morning we were on our way to the railway station when I asked Teresa with sudden premonition, "Where's the play?"

"What play?" said she, looking startled and terrified.

"*The Countess Valeska.*"

"I don't know."

"But you packed it up."

We reached the station, and I looked fearfully through all my bags. No sign of the play.

"You've left it at the hotel," said Teresa.

It was one of Teresa's most aggravating expedients when

danger threatened to retreat behind a statement that the negligence was mine.

"You mean *you* left it behind," I cried. "You must go back at once to the hotel and find it—and don't come near me until you get it. You have ruined me if it is lost. I shall have no play. It's the only copy. I have to produce it in ten days. Go! Leave me and never let me see you again if you don't find it."

The train was about to start, and we were all hustled aboard. Teresa stood on the platform looking petrified. She walked back to the hotel, searched my room and her own but could find no trace of the play. She questioned the manager, who questioned the servants, who questioned one another. Late that afternoon a maid recalled that she had heard a boy in the linen room talking or reading to himself. After much running about the boy was found, and Teresa explained for the hundredth time what the play looked like. It was in four separate parts; each part had a pink cover. The boy admitted having found it in a drawer and read some part of it. He then had thrown it with other rubbish from the various rooms upon the heap of refuse which each morning was removed from the hotel by the dustman.

The contractor for the dustmen told where he had dumped his load. Teresa, accompanied by the boy who had thrown the play away, went to the dump heap, and after a dusty search recovered three acts out of four, badly soaked. But the fourth act—where was that? All day and on into the night she toiled and dug but to no avail. She was there again at daylight when children and ragpickers arrived. One person remembered a child who had picked up a pink book and walked away reading it.

Teresa was led to the child's home at the other end of the city, but the child had given the book to a tailor who lived some distance away. Teresa climbed to the top of a tenement and found the man with the fourth act. He was an eccentric, called "Shakespeare" because he quoted poetry as he sat cross-legged sewing.

Teresa fled with her prize to the station. Without food or money, she talked the station-master into giving her a meal and a free ride on a "loose" engine.

"I'm starving," said Teresa.

"I'll lend you a dollar," said the stationmaster.

"I like you," said Teresa.

She refreshed herself with coffee and doughnuts—then got up on the engine and started away.

She caught a train at the junction and found the conductor was an Irishman. As Teresa later remarked, "I knew I had him as soon as he said, 'Well, my beauty, what's wrong with you?' " She boarded the train without a ticket and invited the conductor to come and see the "show." She reached the theatre in time to dress me for my performance, and was regarded as something between Joan of Arc and Grace Darling, the lighthouse keeper's heroic daughter.

I had arranged to open my New York season at the Knickerbocker Theatre with *As You Like It*, since my production of *The Countess Valeska* was not quite ready.

My management was now in the hands of Charles B. Dillingham, which relieved me of anxiety and enabled me to avail myself of expert advice. Besides I needed aid in finding plays, and

Charles Frohman, who was associated with Mr. Dillingham, could help me greatly there.

Mr. Dillingham begged me not to think of beginning my season with *As You Like It* since Augustin Daly was to produce that play the week before I began.

" 'Let the galled jade wince, my withers are unwrung,' " I quoted and went on with my preparations.

"Why does Mr. Daly play *As You Like It* when you have announced it?" asked a newspaper interviewer. "He opened with *Romeo and Juliet* against you not so long ago."

"You must ask Mr. Daly," said I, and thought of the wager of a dinner between Clarke Davis and the manager.

As You Like It was received well, and then I produced *Valeska*. The press and the public responded finely. I had a good New York engagement and felt that my season was secure. My managers begged me to take full advantage of my success and confine my efforts to the one play for the entire season, letting them advertize it as a novelty. They urged me not to divert public attention by turning to my Shakespeare repertoire.

With a sad heart I acquiesced. Indeed I was compelled to sacrifice inclination to expediency. The time had come when I had to confess that in spite of the loyal support of a cultivated minority, I could hardly make a living out of my productions of Shakespeare's plays. The reviews I had always received from my very first days were all, nay, more than the most praise-greedy woman could ask. But there was the fact—cold and not to be put away—that at the season's end I was always poor. I repeated to myself one of Shakespeare's sonnets. How the words seemed to fit my case—every line—each word—as though it had been written for me.

"Farewell, thou art too dear for my possessing,
And like enough thou know'st thy estimate;
The charter of thy worth gives thee releasing;
My bonds in thee are all eterminate.
For how do I hold thee but by thy granting,
And for that riches where is my deserving?
The cause of this fair gift in me is wanting,
And so my patient back again is swerving.
Thyself thou gav'st, thy own worth then not knowing,
Or me, to whom thou gav'st it, else mistaking;
So thy great gift, upon misprision growing,
Comes home again, on better judgment making.
    Thus have I had thee as a dream doth flatter,
    In sleep a king, but waking no such matter."

Yes, I had had a great happiness, and I determined that it was but for a time I would make concession. The tired businessman, the people who are not aware that Shakespeare is good entertainment, to these I must introduce myself in some guise which would gratify them and allow me, when I had made them my adherents, to lead them with me back to the Forest of Arden.

At the end of that season for the first time in my life I made a deposit in a bank, placing seven hundred dollars to my account.

That summer I went to Paris and as usual saw many plays. There I met Frank Colfax and gave him back the five hundred dollars though he refused to accept the six per cent interest I offered.

I began my next season with *Countess Valeska,* and then I

began to prepare for production *Colinette* by C. Lenotre and Gabrielle Martin. Recently successful in Paris, it was a light and airy affair, and when Charles Frohman saw it on tour he felt that it was too tame to have much prospect of success. Mr. Frohman knew his public well and said I must supply some elements of surprise. I put on my thinking cap.

In one scene the heroine has a secret interview with her husband who is in danger of arrest. In the manuscript they merely embraced as he entered on the scene. I considered the circumstances—her joy, his danger—and I devised some business which created the desired sensation. I was standing at the back of the stage in an alcove as he entered down right. Having placed a chaise longue between my position and the door, I ran and leaped over it and rushed into his arms.

Colinette served my purposes for the entire season. Since my contract with my new management provided me with a certainty each week and a share in the profits, I was free from anxiety. But with the royalty on the play and the various expenses of production deducted, the profits were not large.

During this season Mr. Beerbohm Tree negotiated with Charles Frohman for my services in Stephen Phillips's *Ulysses* at Her Majesty's Theatre in London, but I was not able to accept as I had other plans far in advance.

Next Mr. Frohman contracted with Clyde Fitch to write a play for me. The playwright chose Barbara Frietchie for his heroine and set to work.

Barbara Frietchie * was produced in New York in 1899 and

---

* The play was of course based on the Whittier ballad in which ninety-year-old Barbara Frietchie was represented as hanging out the Union flag from her window in Frederick town and defying the Confederate general, Stonewall Jackson, with:

proved to be a most gratifying success. However, like all my new plays it met with rebuke from those who bewailed my secession from Shakespeare.

————

"Shoot, if you must, this old gray head,
But spare your country's flag," she said.

Mr. Fitch exercised dramatic license to rejuvenate Barbara Frietchie and allowed Miss Marlowe, playing the title part, to appear as a charming Maryland belle in her own brown tresses.

chapter 14

Knighthood Flowers

The early nineteen hundreds were the day of the historical romantic play. *The Prisoner of Zenda* made a great success in England and in America, *The Forest Lovers, Alice of Old Vincennes, Under the Red Robe, Rupert of Hentzau,* and *The Three Musketeers* were filling theatres all over the country. But *When Knighthood Was in Flower* outdistanced them all.

The book on which the play was based was a novel by Charles Major, an Indiana lawyer. Its sale of half a million copies heightened the competition for its dramatic rights. Luckily I secured them after my friend, Morris Ross, persuaded the author to journey to St. Louis to see me act Rosalind in *As You Like It.*

Charles Frohman engaged Guy Carlton to dramatize the novel, but in spite of that dramatist's considerable experience, I could not accept the play he submitted. To me it was a hopeless piece of work. What was I to do? *Barbara Frietchie* could not possibly serve me for another season, so I decided that I dared not go away and leave my fortunes to accident. I canceled my passage to Europe and summoned Paul Kester to my aid.

I rented a small house at Highmount in the Catskills for my mother and myself, and Mr. Kester joined us there to write an entirely new version of the novel. For two months we lived, breathed and talked of nothing else than Mary Tudor, heroine of the Major novel. Mr. Kester seized at once on all the vital and essential aspects of the story, and with an unfailing instinct he swiftly composed his scenario and arranged his material. He would work all day, and after we had discussed what had been done he would sit up half the night engrossed in his task. In eight weeks he had evolved an admirable drama. Constant in action and suspense, his script added incident and dialogue but preserved the integrity of the book. I would read aloud the scenes as they reached completion and impersonate the characters as I had schooled myself to do in my earlier days. My enthusiasm grew with the growth of the play, and at last we both felt that the thing had been accomplished and that I had about as "starry" a part as anyone could aspire to. Indeed Mary Tudor was on the stage from the rise of the curtain in each of the four acts till its fall. Every mood of all the characters I had ever played seemed packed into its compass. The public wanted "pep," and here it was by the bucket and cartload. It was fortunate that I felt well and vital, for this play which needed an actress sound in wind and limb, set a pace for me. The effect of the action on my company was evident; there was no lolling about; all the cast was alert.

At the end of Act II, King Henry VIII has sent the Bishop of London to demand that Mary Tudor wed the French King. She is in love with Charles Brandon and angrily refuses. The bishop, perturbed, protests and threatens while Mary defies him. At length the bishop asks, "What answer shall I take to your brother, the King of England?" And Mary, who is rushing off up a staircase, turns in fury and cries, "Say to the King my brother that I will see him and his Kingdom sunk in hell before I'll marry Louis of France!"

The ladies and gentlemen of my company, many of the old-fashioned, Shakespearean veterans, felt that there was impro-

priety in that utterance and suggested the public might find it
a trifle candid. But I reasoned that the propriety of any utterance depends upon the circumstances under which it is spoken,
and the speech remained unaltered.

When the first night arrived, the play went like a whirlwind
from start to finish. From the moment Mary Tudor entered I
felt assured and in high feather I went from act to act with
spirits unbounded and unflagging. The play was bringing within
my grasp all I had longed for through so many hard-working
years. Freedom, independence, the right to choose without
restraint. That greatest of all blessings, the direction of my own
will, and the right to seek happiness in my own way. How I
had waited, longed for this moment! As the curtain rose and
fell the audience applauded and finally broke out into cheers.
My whole body throbbed with the exertion and the sense of
victory. I saw far into the days to come. I saw my dear object
accomplished—my return to Shakespeare's heroines, welcomed
by those very people.

Many felt that *Knighthood* was not a worthy vehicle for me,
but I left splitting of hairs to the philosophers. The box office
was stormed. Wherever I went, my advance sale was fifteen or
twenty thousand dollars. Crowds waited outside the stage door
to see me and take my hand. Policemen had to make a path for
me through the multitude. "Don't kill the woman!" yelled a
blue-coated Hercules one night as I tried to make my way to
my cab. My orchestra was driven from its usual place to sit
under the stage and fiddle in obscurity; their space was needed
for extra rows of seats.

On the first night at the Knickerbocker in New York, Charles

Frohman sent me a card after the first act on which he had written, "Splendid! Wonderful! You have nothing to worry about for the next five years." I was able to send him a telegram from Chicago with the proud legend that I had played to more money than the Rogers Brothers.*

My first season of *Knighthood* made me a fortune sufficient to render me independent for the rest of my life. The second season I more than doubled it. Freedom was mine.

After two years I could stand the strain of Mary Tudor no more. The unceasing activity of the part told on me, and I had to seek less arduous roles. I could no doubt have played the character for five years as Mr. Frohman had predicted, but my soul cried out for fresh air, and I looked for a new play.

Never shall I belittle *Knighthood*. To have contempt for an entertainment is also to have it for people who enjoyed the play as a wholesome recreation. I have no sense of shame that I played it. I put into it all that I had ever learned and while I acted it, I gave audiences every particle of strength and ability I possessed.

With some of the profits I built myself a pretty house at Highmount near the spot where Mr. Kester had written the play. I also acquired a residence in New York, and I began to feel that I had taken root in the world.

Knighthood had flowered splendidly, but the next seed I planted in my dramatic garden had hardly sprouted before it wilted. In my desperate search for a new play I had not chosen carefully enough.

* Max and Gus Rogers, comedians, played in a series of popular revues: *The Rogers Brothers in Ireland,*——*at Harvard,*——*in Wall Street,* etc.

Toward the end of 1901 I was in despair of ever finding a suitable play for the coming year. I could see absolutely nothing on the horizon, no drama possessing sufficient dignity and beauty.

Then in a Washington manicure shop I read a copy of the French pictorial paper, *L'Illustration*, which described a play called *Queen Fiametta*, then running with success in Paris. The author was Catulle Mendez. I read its synopsis and was impressed with it; it seemed to have qualities of romance and charm. I secured the rights, had a translation made and induced Paul Kester to smooth the dialogue.

But Frank Colfax, my stage manager, foretold failure for the play when he was consulted by Paul who affectionately called him "The Commodore."

"They won't have this *Queen Fiametta*," Frank predicted. "They'll jump on it in every way, shape and manner."

"Don't you think it's a good part for Miss Marlowe?" Mr. Kester asked.

"No, it ain't."

"Why not?"

"Too much religion. People won't stand for it."

"It made a great success in Paris."

"New York ain't Paris, Mr. Kester."

"Well, Commodore, you ought to be a good judge of a play."

"If I ain't, who is?" Frank demanded. "I've seen everything for the last fifty years."

"What would be *your* idea of a play, Commodore?"

"Why, *Monte Cristo*. I saw Jim O'Neil in it at the Baldwin Theatre in San Francisco. Now there's a play. Jim jumped off a rock set piece thirty foot high into the sea."

"A fine part, no doubt."

"The people used to stand up and yell," Frank recalled. "I tell you, actors in them days could act."

"And jump too, evidently," added Mr. Kester.

"People won't stand for all that talk about the church," Frank repeated.

"But how about the love story?" the playwright inquired.

"Immaterial, inconsequent and irrelevant," pronounced Colfax.

And Frank was right. The play did arouse religious controversy. I produced it in Boston, played it there for two weeks and for two more in Providence. Then both Charles Frohman and Paul Kester advised me to take it off and close my season, and I obeyed. Frank Colfax was entitled to the satisfaction of saying, "I told you so," which no doubt is one of humanity's most gratifying experiences.

I had bought the rights to George W. Cable's novel, *The Cavalier,** a Civil War story like *Barbara Frietchie*. Paul Kester, anxious to help me recoup my *Fiametta* losses, issued me an invitation.

"Come down to Woodlawn and stay with my mother. I think I can have the play of *The Cavalier* ready in four weeks. I know a man who can help me. He will write the dialogue while I construct the play."

* "The Southern girl . . . goes to the front, and there is one scene where in a boxcar made into a telegraph office, Julia Marlowe had the first opportunity of her career to utilize what she had learned as a girl in the telegraph school at Cincinnati. The regular operator being sick or shot or something, the heroine in the emergency must click out a message herself, a message upon which the plot turns, and Miss Marlowe astonished the telegraphers in the audience by clicking it out correctly."—C. E. Russell.

I promptly accepted for I was in need of rest, and the reception of my latest venture had distressed me greatly. At the Kester home in West Virginia, an old colonial house built by Lawrence Washington, I sat down and waited while Paul for the second time gave me of his industry and devotion to turn defeat into victory. In four weeks he completed *The Cavalier*, aided by George Middleton. It was practically a new story, with much incident added to the original. I tried the play in New Haven and then went to New York where we met with great success, running for twelve weeks at the Criterion Theatre. My season on the road proved equally fortunate.

On the first night of *The Cavalier* occurred one of those contretemps which emphasize Oliver Wendell Holmes's advice never to be as funny as one can.

George W. Cable, gratified at the success of this dramatization of his book, was persuaded to step before the curtain. Greeted with great applause, he addressed the audience: "Ladies and Gentlemen, I am drunk——" Here he paused fatally. Whether he expected laughter and was disconcerted because it did not materialize, or whether he was indeed at a loss for words, he became embarrassed and repeated his alarming assertion. The assemblage held its breath as the distinguished gentleman reassured them as to his lamentable condition, and at length completed his sentence by saying, "I am drunk with delight at your appreciation." But it was too late. The audience did not recover, and the author retired amid silent wonder.

chapter 15

Enter Mr. Sothern *

No longer was Shakespeare "too dear for my possessing." The time seemed ripe for me to claim him again, for I had earned my following and my independence.

I was eager to produce plays I selected in the most admirable fashion possible, not only fine scenically but with a company of the most capable actors I could procure. The more I considered the matter, however, the more I was convinced that the enterprise would gain both in excellence and in drawing power if I could associate myself with a co-star who would lend distinction to the male parts. Such an association would enlarge my repertoire of plays, and I could then produce *The*

---

* Edward Hugh Sothern, son of Mr. and Mrs. Edward Askew Sothern, was born in New Orleans in 1859 during one of his actor father's American tours. Educated in England, he turned from a career as an artist to follow the paternal footsteps in the theatre. His New York debut in 1879 was ruined by an attack of stage fright so paralyzing that he could not speak his lines. However, he persisted and after considerable stock-company experience made a great success in such cloak-and-sword dramas as *The Prisoner of Zenda* and *If I Were King*. In a highly popular revival he played a role created by his father, Lord Dundreary in *Our American Cousin*. In 1896, he married his leading lady, Virginia Harned; they were divorced in 1911.

Walter Prichard Eaton in an article in *The Dictionary of American Biography* praises Sothern's bodily grace, his well-trained voice, his swordplay and portrayal of dashing heroics, and his skill as a stage director. "He was not by natural endowment a tragic actor, but he was led by ambition and by devotion to the ideal of a classic repertoire to act Hamlet, Shylock, Macbeth and Antony and by dint of hard work and keen, sensitive intelligence he gave in nearly all cases an excellent account of himself. His best Shakespearean role, however, was probably Malvolio, where with no loss of comic effect he presented a pathetic picture of an inherent gentleman overcome by vanity."

Merchant of Venice, Macbeth and other dramas, difficult to cast without a distinguished confrere.

Henry Irving and Ellen Terry were a happy combination. So were Edwin Booth, Lawrence Barrett and Madame Modjeska. In their case and others the gain to the public was great and the ventures both fruitful artistically and fortunate financially. My thought at once turned toward E. H. Sothern.* It was true that at that time Mr. Sothern had played but one Shakespearean part, and when I heard that he was about to produce *Hamlet*, I, as was the case with many a wiseacre, felt grave doubts as to the possible success of one who had achieved his popularity in light comedy. I had seen him in *The Highest Bidder, Lord Chumley, Lettarblair,* and in his earliest success with Miss

---

* In the following footnote by Mr. Sothern, he refers to himself as "the editor" though actually the author.—F.D.

The editor chokes to record his own excellence, but the heroine of these memoirs demands historical accuracy. However, the historian must declare that any favor extracted from the critical concerning his Shakespearean efforts is due much more to his association with and his instruction by Julia Marlowe than to any qualities of his own, so that in celebrating himself he is paying a tribute to her. The loving and exhaustive labor which she had bestowed upon Shakespearean plays was now lavished upon his own budding endeavor with a generosity and eagerness which he was sane enough to receive hungrily and to profit by with enthusiasm. Very conscious of his own lack of experience in this branch of his calling, he gratefully acknowledges this debt which fortifies his immaturity and his understanding with the hard-won wisdom of painful years.

The propriety or the impropriety of discussing one's own accomplishment under these circumstances has been very prettily debated by Shakespeare himself.

> Oh! how thy worth with manners may I sing,
> When thou art all the better part of me?
> What can mine own praise to mine own self bring
> And what is but mine own when I praise thee?

In this instance the editor, writing as Miss Marlowe, speaks of himself, and, speaking of himself, declares he is speaking for her. While speaking for her, he pays himself certain compliments, which he protests are compliments to Miss Marlowe who, in her own person, he presents as confessing how admirable is the editor. This is what Sir Toby Belch might call the very "license of ink."

Helen Dauvray, *One of Our Girls*. I had also followed his transi-
tion into the realm of romance in *An Enemy to the King, Lady
Ursula, Change Alley, D'Artagnan, The Sunken Bell,* and *If I
Were King*. But although this progress was unusual, I was not
prepared for the step which he undoubtedly achieved when he
produced *Hamlet*. True the touchy Willie Winter demanded
in his review, "What can you expect of a man who goes to sea
in a teaspoon?" But the reception of the performance indicated
the entire change of method of which Mr. Sothern had proved
himself capable.

Friends warned against the dangers of collision of two stars
moving in one orbit, but in the end I decided that if Mr. Sothern were willing to join his forces with my own, I would make
assurance doubly sure and take a bond of Fate.

I therefore deputed Charles Dillingham, my manager, to
approach Mr. Sothern who proved to be eager to devote himself to Shakespearean roles and gladly embraced the opportunity. We met for the first time and soon agreed on all details
of our association. We concluded to produce three plays a
year for three years. The first year's repertoire would be *Hamlet,
Romeo and Juliet* and *Much Ado About Nothing,* for I was now
convinced that I could play Beatrice to advantage. We resolved
to carry out our separate plans for the coming season and to
begin our operations in 1904–5. This matter adjusted, I went
abroad for my holiday.

Meantime Mr. Sothern called to see Charles Frohman on
quite an unrelated matter and when about to take his leave he
asked the manager what he thought of the arrangement he and
I had reached. Mr. Frohman expressed the greatest confidence
in it and asked, "What do you expect?"

Mr. Sothern named a sum which even the most hopeful would have hesitated to believe a possible profit for a Shakespearean enterprise. He added that he expected that both I and he would make that sum each year of our association.

"I'll give it to you—make it a certainty—if you'll let me manage you," Mr. Frohman offered.

"For three years?"

"Yes, for three years. How many weeks will you play?"

"Forty weeks each season."

"Done," said Mr. Frohman.

Mr. Frohman undertook to be responsible for all the many details of production: the costumes, scenery and properties on a lavish scale, with the entire stage management in the hands of Mr. Sothern and myself. My co-star cabled me about the offer, and I willingly accepted.

I am persuaded that Charles Frohman's chief motive in making his proposal was his belief that our adventure was going to be first-class in every respect for the public and the best interest of the drama. His generosity cannot be acknowledged with sufficient appreciation. He permitted us every possible freedom in expenditure and the large sums of money which he guaranteed to pay both of us would in the estimation of less courageous managers have left small margin for profit. However, it is gratifying to state that he did profit by the transaction for the two seasons it remained in effect. At the end of the second year when he wished to send us on a tour of forty weeks of one-night stands, we both felt that such a strain—at least seven performances a week of the heaviest roles an actor can assume—would be a really dangerous undertaking. We therefore asked Mr. Frohman to release us from our contract for the third year and undertook our own management. From that time, with the lapse of two seasons when we resumed our separate repertoires, we shouldered the responsibility of our own company, and our venture was favored by the enthusiastic support of the country.

That the public responds generously when their confidence in the quality of the offering has been established, the record of our own enterprise makes clear. For more than twenty years we were blessed with good fortune and most generous appreciation. The labor involved was extreme, but the satisfaction was very great indeed. Mr. Sothern's long experience as a producer and stage manager (from his earliest days he always directed his own productions down to the minutest details) relieved me of drudgery and fatigue. I was able to leave everything of that nature with confidence in his hands and, saving my strength, devote myself to the contemplation and execution of my roles only.

Each year we put on three great Shakespearean productions, elaborate to a degree in scenery, costumes and musical accompaniment, and drilled a large company with numbers of supernumeraries, trained to intricate co-operation. That work was accomplished without undue haste, with premeditation, foreknowledge, precision and good humor, calmly, perfectly and within the space of four weeks. Think of it! Three new productions in four weeks! Nothing was left to chance, but we had a reason ready for any doubtful or disputed point.

I had been informed by gossipmongers, of whom there is ever a goodly crop on hand, that Mr. Sothern was a difficult person with whom to work, that he was martinet, that he had been known to swear with considerable violence. Indeed he was said to be equipped with a really admirable vocabulary of picturesque adjectives. That did not alarm me, for I recalled a learned professor, given to exhibitions of impatience, who found it soothed his nerves to call his opponent an "isosceles triangle."

It appeared subsequently that Mr. Sothern, too, had been advised that I was as difficult to get on with as a woman could well be, that I was never on time and that I had an opinion of my own from which it was extremely difficult to separate me.

Mr. Sothern approached me on that matter at one of our earliest meetings with an admirable candor I have since learned to respect. He said, "Miss Marlowe, I am sure you have heard that I am a difficult fellow to get on with, and I have heard that you have quite a will of your own. So I want to say at the earliest possible moment, so as to remove from your mind any apprehensions that we may not agree—I want to promise you that you shall have *my* way in everything."

It was said with so great an air of concession and sincere consideration for my welfare that for the moment I did not observe the pronoun. So I smiled sweetly and thanked Mr. Sothern for his gallantry.

"Did you hear what he said?" a friend asked as I walked away.

"Yes," I said. "How kind, how considerate."

"But he said you should have *his* way."

I reflected. So he did! Well, we'll see. But in the end I found Mr. Sothern's way was usually the simple and direct one to save time and reach the result, so I was content.

Many of my friends were astonished that I should consent

to play Ophelia, a character new to me. Quite apart from the fact that I perceived that our association must be cemented by a considerable willingness to give and take, I considered Ophelia to be one of Shakespeare's greatest female characters. It would be most ungracious for me to speak of other Ophelias, but evidently in many cases the men who attempted Hamlet entrusted the role to the second juvenile woman of the company. The leading woman usually persuaded herself that the part, being short, was not worthy of her talents. I felt strongly the appeal of the "Rose of May" and was eager to embody her.

We once, however, met an Ophelia who had succeeded in discounting Hamlet completely. When she called on Mr. Sothern to seek an engagement in our company, he asked, "Have you had any experience in Shakespeare's plays?"

"Oh, yes," she said. "I have played Ophelia."

"Who was the Hamlet?"

"I forget," came the answer.

Mr. Sothern's preparation for playing the Melancholy Dane was thorough and strenuous. To show the skill in swordplay demanded by the text for the fight with Laertes, he took lessons from Senac, a distinguished fencing coach, and practiced disarming his opponent by a difficult feat of arms. He planned to engage and bind Laertes's blade with his own, toss it into the air, catch it with his left hand and gallantly return it. However, considerable dexterity is required for such a maneuver, and after weeks of rehearsing Mr. Sothern doubted he could accomplish it with any certainty. He therefore abandoned it and arranged to beat Laertes's rapier from his grasp, place a foot upon it as it clattered to the floor and proffer his own weapon to his disarmed adversary.

But on the first night at the Garden Theatre, New York, the carefully prepared bout got out of hand, though Mr. Sternroyd, playing Laertes, was himself a capable fencer. Mr. Sothern, unable to give directions that might be overheard by the audience, grew more and more anxious as Sternroyd became confused. At length Hamlet beat down Laertes's blade so violently that it struck the stage on its tip and bounded aloft six or eight feet. Without looking up Mr. Sothern instinctively raised his left hand to ward off the blow expected on his head. Lo and behold, the rapier's hilt descended directly into his open hand which clutched it and brandished it high. With an actor's instinct he recognized what he had done and held the pose for seconds, then extended his own blade to Laertes. Deafening applause greeted the splendid swordsmanship.

After the play, a fencing professor sent in his card, and Mr. Sothern received him on the stage.

"I have written a book on fencing," said the visitor. "I shall be grateful if you will allow me to dedicate it to you and if you will write a preface. I have never seen such skill."

"And never will again," the candid Mr. Sothern stated. "It was an accident."

The professor would not believe him, and it took much argument to convince him.

Too often bad luck seems to follow good. At a later performance Mr. Sothern, in disarming Laertes, struck down the latter's weapon so that its point pierced Hamlet's shoe and tore away a toe-nail. For six weeks he played with his foot in bandages and finally was compelled to submit to an operation which sent him to the hospital for two weeks. Discharged, he resumed his work, but blood poisoning set in and after ten weeks of treatment it was necessary to remove the toe joint. On recovery he continued his tour in *Hamlet* only to have the Cincinnati Grand Opera House catch fire during his performance.

The fire started from waste paper too near a red-hot stove under the stage. Mr. Sothern had reached the moment of Hamlet's first soliloquy, "Oh, that this too, too solid flesh would melt," when at that appropriate cue a great tongue of flame leaped through an iron grating in the middle of the auditorium.

The house was not greatly crowded, but a panic would have ensued if Mr. Sothern had not stepped to the footlights and quietly begged those at the back of the house to make their exit through the doors to the street and those near the front to come forward and be assisted over the footlights to make their exit by the stage door. He then asked the musicians to play, which they did with calm and courage.

Suddenly came a shout from the gallery, "We are locked in!" An attendant had locked the door to prevent any free admission and gone away.

The people in the gallery, seeing the smoke and flame increase, threatened to jump. Men yelled and women screamed, while those below delayed their retreat and some who had climbed on to the stage stood to watch. Fortunately a fire house was next door to the theatre, separated only by an alley with a covered bridge connecting with the theatre gallery. Firemen hacked down doors with axes just in time to prevent many from jumping to the floor below. All occupants of the gallery escaped across the bridge. Meanwhile those at the back of the auditorium had reached the street and those in front walked leisurely across the stage to make their escape.

As Mr. Sothern, the last man, emerged from the building

the entire stage gave way and fell into a seething furnace of flame. He and the rest of the company walked back in costume to their hotel.

Next morning a bellboy knocked at Mr. Sothern's door and announced that there were several gentlemen who desired to see him. "Who are they?" he asked. "I don't know, sir," said the boy, "but they all have spears in their hands." They proved to be the *Hamlet* supers. There they stood, twenty-four of them, dressed in ancient chain armor and gray-green tights, cloaks of black and gray stripes. They wore steel helmets and were carrying ten-foot spears. Mr. Sothern marched them and forty other supers across the street to a ready-made clothing store and provided them all with entire outfits from shoes to hats.

Henry Miller telegraphed a kind offer of the loan of the costumes and sets of his own production of *Hamlet,* and within two days Mr. Sothern was able to open again at the Town Hall.

Incidentally the Opera House which was destroyed was the theatre where I had made my first appearance on the boards when I went on as a child supernumerary.

Before Mr. Sothern and I began to co-star I produced *Fools of Nature,* a modern comedy hardly suited to my purpose. I only played it six weeks on tour and finished the season with revivals of *Ingomar* and *When Knighthood Was in Flower.* Mr. Sothern produced *The Proud Prince* by Justin McCarthy, a version of the fable of Robert of Sicily, in which he achieved a great success with a magnificent and costly production.

During the summer we began preparations for our three Shakespeare plays. A fine company was engaged. The costumes were carefully designed by Karl of London and executed by Herman of New York. As I have already said, Mr. Frohman was lavish in his aid. I went away for a rest with a happy heart, looking forward to three years of acting Shakespeare.

I had wandered far afield yet always with this end in view. But I had gained in experience and in the actor's craft, and I believed I was more capable than ever before of doing justice to the poet I adored.

chapter 16

To Shakespeare's London

When the forces of the drama and of literature are united, as in the case of Shakespeare's plays, one may look forward to exhibitions of temperament.

That was apparently the expectation of one of the officials of the Knickerbocker Theatre in New York where we began rehearsals of our three plays. As he stood contemplating the peaceful proceedings, he looked with fine scorn at Frank Colfax and said, "There's too much 'if you please' and 'thank you' in this company," and left the scene, convinced of the hopelessness of such tame operations. Nevertheless, our work went on with swiftness and precision and a knowledge of something daily accomplished, something done. That was fortunate, for as I have said, the task of preparing three great plays at the same time within a period of four weeks was difficult.

For my part I had one new role in Ophelia; Juliet and Beatrice I had played before. Mr. Sothern had to appear in two new characters: Romeo and Benedick, in addition to shouldering the heavier part of the stage management.

However, we opened in Chicago with *Romeo and Juliet* under the most favorable circumstances. A great audience welcomed this union of effort of two actors who had pleased them in many plays. The press responded with appreciation which gave us much confidence in the future. Our performances of *Hamlet* and *Much Ado About Nothing* were also received with great satisfaction. The success of our Chicago engagement was repeated in New York, and our tour of the country realized my highest hopes.

The second season under Mr. Frohman's management we produced *The Merchant of Venice, The Taming of the Shrew* and *Twelfth Night.* Portia was a new role for me, as also was Katharine in the *Shrew.* Shylock, Petruchio and Malvolio were all three new characters for Mr. Sothern. Our treatment of the *Shrew* drew forth some "odorous" comparisons with the production by Augustin Daly, since we elected to play the piece as a farce and chose to omit the Introduction. Those decisions gave rise to much lively comment and displays of erudition and ultimately to the admission that our manner of treating the play added considerable merriment. Although some precedents had been smashed, our innovations were not greatly deplored.

Tradition sometimes misleads her votaries. In the *Merchant of Venice* it had long been the custom for actors to improve (as they imagined) Shylock's opportunity at the conclusion of Act II, Scene 5, by giving him words spoken by Salanio in a subsequent scene, namely the speech:

> My daughter!—O my ducats!—O my daughter!
> Fled with a Christian!—O my Christian ducats!—
> Justice! The law! My ducats and my daughter!
> A sealed bag, two sealed bags of ducats,
> Of double ducats stolen from me by my daughter!
> And jewels—two stones, two rich and precious stones!
> Stolen by my daughter!—Justice find the girl!
> She hath the stones upon her, and the ducats!

Salanio, of course, speaks these lines in mockery of Shylock, and to his companion Salarino. But the ambitious actor of Shylock would return on the scene after Jessica's elopement, enter the house, discover the theft and bewail the loss in those transposed words.

We did not take that liberty. Mr. Sothern as Shylock merely returned after the laughing elopers had gone and stood waiting by his door. There were some wiselings who resented it on the grounds that Mr. Sothern had tampered with the text and cut out some of Shylock's most effective speeches. It was too easy a victory to point out the facts, so we did not notice the matter at all.

In a similar manner the church scene in *Much Ado About Nothing* concludes with Benedick's words to Beatrice: "Go, comfort your cousin: I must say she is dead: and so, farewell." *Exeunt*. But adventurous souls had arranged that as the two were about to exeunt, Beatrice should call, "Benedick!" *He halts*. "Yes?" "You'll kill him?" cries Beatrice. "I swear it." "You'll kill him—you'll kill him dead?" "As sure as he's alive, I will."

For that there is, of course, no warrant whatever. It is a barefaced invention. Yet we were denounced on occasion for mauling the sacred text by omitting what never existed. We concluded the scene as written, adding the permissible pantomime that Benedick and Beatrice impetuously embrace at "and so farewell."

Louis de Foe, the dramatic critic of the New York *World*, was one of those most opposed to our rendition of the *Taming of the Shrew*. Later, however, he frankly admitted that he had been convinced that our interpretation was to be preferred and was vindicated by the text.

On the first night of this play in New York, Herbert Satterlee and his family were seated in a box. When Petruchio scatters the plates and dishes and cries, "What's this—mutton? 'Tis burnt and so is all the meat. What dogs are these?" He flings the leg of mutton at the terrified servitors who stand in a trembling group in the corner near the proscenium. The mutton missed the varlets and struck Mr. Satterlee square on his white shirt front. With great presence of mind and fine aim he flung it back and hit the cook on the head, adding one touch of nature to the hilarious occasion.

While performing *The Taming of the Shrew*, I met with a painful accident, spraining my ankle so badly it had to be placed in a plaster cast. Here was a dilemma. The active and constant movement of the play demanded that I should be here, there and everywhere with swift movement.

Mr. Sothern was equal to the occasion. He had a wooden chair constructed which could be carried like a sedan chair by poles attached to each side. When Katharine first appeared she was discovered seated and never stirred from her place except to rise and sit in one spot, aided by the various wedding guests. When the moment arrived for Petruchio to carry her off, he called to his followers who brought on the new chair. They seized Katharine and tied her into it. Thus she was carried away, and in that chair she remained for the rest of the play, lifted everywhere—over tables, through doors, up to bed and down again. Sleeping, waking, railing and finally laughing, she lived a hectic, perambulatory existence.

The new device was greeted as a happy invention in town after town, and no one suspected it as the expedient it was.

That device was more easily carried out in *Twelfth Night* and *The Merchant of Venice*. I subsequently saw Madame Bernhardt play after her leg had been amputated. It was wonderful how little one considered the lack of movement, since eyes were concentrated entirely on her face.

My dear Parson Price was greatly excited when Mr. Sothern and I combined our forces. He had in his earliest days in New York been in the same company with Mr. Sothern's father whom he remembered with affection, and he always called the son "the boy." My co-star now became a pupil as I had been. He had a grand piano placed on the stage and found time every evening before getting ready for his performance to take an hour's lesson. During our New York season he greatly improved his voice and vocal endurance.

No matter how much care is devoted to the training of supernumeraries, accidents will happen.

Mr. Sothern had rehearsed the fight between the Montagues and the Capulets in *Romeo and Juliet* with the greatest minuteness, all the business being carefully considered and each separate action perfected with endless pains. Nevertheless one Biondi, an Italian who played the mandolin, nearly ruined the first performance in St. Louis. Each person in the conflict was given exact ejaculations and even words to utter which in the confusion of the melee would not be heard but which would give the effect of a violent quarrel. Biondi had many such exclamations of challenge and battle, but since he spoke broken English, Mr. Sothern was careful to place him at the back of the stage where no utterance of his could possibly be distinguished in the general outcry. But on this occasion Biondi was seized by an inspiration. With the stuffed club he had been using to belabor a Capulet raised in menace above his head, he jumped into the middle of the stage, as the outraged Prince Escalus of Verona and his suite entered to subdue the combatants. When the Prince cried:

> Rebellious subjects, enemies to peace,
> Profaners of this neighbor-stained steel,
> Will they not hear? What ho! You men, you beasts!

the terrible Biondi yelled, "Down with the Irish!" But before the audience had time to laugh, he was seized by other characters and, overwhelmed by numbers, was smothered into oblivion.

On another memorable night a conscientious super did his best to carry out instructions and was only defeated in his good intentions after a considerable conflict.

In rehearsing the extra people to lend variety to their cries and shouts, Mr. Sothern would give each one a line, unheard in the general clamor but giving the effect of unanimous acclaim. Unless instructed with such care, people told to shout will with one voice cry, "Oh" or "Hi!" in unison. Mr. Sothern to give variety to the cries ordered three or four to say, "A," with others calling out "E," "I," "O," and "U," thus providing all the vowel sounds. The effect was excellent. But one conscientious fellow determined to outdo all his rivals. One night he planted himself in the center of the stage near the footlights, glared at the audience and began to shout at the top of his voice the entire complement of vowels. When Mr. Sothern later asked him to explain, he disarmingly replied, "Say, Boss, you told me to shout all the vowels, and I just wanted to please you."

Another innovation we introduced was to provide in the front of the theatre a uniformed attendant who would offer his services to those customers who could not obtain the seats they desired at the box office. It is to be admitted that the man in the box office does often have his patience tried, but on the other hand it is not entirely a criminal offence that a nervous woman or an absent-minded man does not for the moment know his or her own mind. With a long line of other persons, more or less in haste, behind the person questioning the box office man as to price and location, the ticket buyer is apt to become confused and leave baffled. At that unhappy moment our man would approach politely and offer to show the location of seats. "I don't want the fifteenth row," the customer might say. "Allow me to show you how near it is to the stage," our man would suggest. If the seats proved satisfactory, our agent would procure them for the customer. The plan worked quite well, but our "Information Man" told us that the chief question propounded by most ladies was, "How old is Miss Marlowe?" It was taken for granted that he was there to supply biographical details concerning cast and company.

By a strange coincidence when we played Cincinnati, appearing in the rebuilt Grand Opera House, there was again an alarm of fire. I was about to begin the potion scene in *Romeo and Juliet* when I heard that ominous movement of the entire audience which is the first danger sign.

I went at once to the footlights and asked, "Please, what is the matter?" and a voice replied, "There's a smell of smoke out here." I called Mr. Sothern who was, as always, standing in the wings. He came on the stage and ordered the house lights to be raised. A man who occupied a private box now stood up and said, "I am here in this box with my wife and children. The smoke is leaking through the wall from the next building into our box, but we don't intend to start a panic. We intend to sit here until Mr. Sothern tells us we are in danger." There was applause at that, and at the same moment the theatre fireman came on the stage, held up the hand of authority and announced, "There ain't no danger—see?" He explained that a faulty flue next door was the sole trouble, and there was much smoke without any fire.

We rearranged our lights and lowered the curtain in the hope of regaining the illusion of the scene. Then the curtain went up and poor Juliet began once more, "Ay, those attires are best . . ." Soon the magic words had their effect, and our audience was with us.

For many years I had strongly desired to play in London. Two or three times I had come near doing so, notably when Beerbohm Tree and George Alexander invited me. I had spoken of my ambition to Mr. Frohman, but he had advised against it. He had two theatres in London and was familiar with conditions there, and from a money point of view I was aware that his reasons were excellent. There was no doubt that my best fortunes lay in the country where I had a reputation. Few American actors playing Shakespeare had been able to draw paying houses in London. Edwin Booth played at the Princess Theatre to mere handfuls of people. Helena Modjeska had no better fortune at the Haymarket Theatre. Fanny Daven-

port could make no way at all. John McCullough played at
Drury Lane to a corporal's guard. Many years ago Joseph Jefferson had filled a poorly attended engagement in London and
strongly counselled me against a like adventure. Mary Anderson, perhaps alone of all our legitimate actors, had won a
signal victory under Henry Abbey's management at the Lyceum
Theatre. Laurence Barrett had a disastrous experience, and
Richard Mansfield found no success and returned to his American admirers with bitter thoughts of London Town.

My reasons were sentimental, I suppose, but I still wanted
to play Shakespearc in Shakespeare's town. I wanted the approval of the people among whom I had been born.

Mr. Sothern had in his apprentice years played in London
with Charles Wyndham, with John S. Clarke, and in the same
company with Richard Mansfield at the Royalty Theatre. He
was familiar with conditions there and knew the chances were
against financial success. He was willing, nevertheless, to risk
the undertaking. When we left Mr. Frohman's management,
and Lee Shubert undertook our booking arrangements, we concluded an agreement with him to play at the Waldorf Theatre,
then under his management. It was not a good theatre for our
purpose, for it was little known; even London cabmen did not
always know where it was. However, we contracted to play there
for six weeks in 1906. On consideration we thought it wise that
we should not depend entirely on our Shakespearean plays
but should begin with a novelty. Therefore during the season
of 1905–6 we produced *The Sunken Bell* by Gerhart Haupt-
mann in which Mr. Sothern had previously appeared. We obtained Percy MacKaye's drama, *Jeanne d'Arc*, from Mrs.
Patrick Campbell for whom it had been written. We prepared

a new production of *When Knighthood Was in Flower*. We placed in rehearsal also a version of *The Daughter of Jorio* by Gabriele D'Annunzio and secured the rights to the same author's *Francesca da Rimini*. Those latter two plays, however, we did not finally produce.

In addition we arranged to take abroad *Romeo and Juliet, Hamlet, Twelfth Night* and *As You Like It,* seven plays in all. We played our American tour as usual until March, when we sailed for England.

As a precaution we arranged our affairs so that we would have a sum in our London bank sufficient to pay our expenses in case not one solitary Londoner should honor us with his company. Said Mr. Sothern, "Let us look at it this way. If one man comes in, that will be on the side of profit." So with the hope of persuading this unknown and solitary individual we deposited in our London bank forty thousand dollars. The expenses of our company would be about five thousand dollars a week for the six weeks. The transportation to London of our company of seventy people including our American working staff and the scenery, properties, and various accoutrements for our seven plays had been paid aside from this London account. In case the longed-for one man could not be lured into our theatre, we would have a good margin with which to return to our native land unwept, unhonored and unsung. But we did attract the one man and quite a large number of others besides. We spent only fifteen thousand out of our forty thousand dollars, so that it may be said that our invasion of England cost us about twenty thousand dollars.

What did we purchase for that sum? The good opinion of several people whose respect we valued highly. I, personally, gratified a desire which had always been troubling my heart ever since I made my first success on the stage. I do not think I ever played with more enthusiasm than I did to our small London audiences. Our plays did not all meet with approval, but we were treated with great consideration and on the last night of our engagement a large number of people came uninvited through the door which led from the front of the house on to the stage to tell us that they had liked our work and to say kind words of cheer and encouragement.

Herbert Beerbohm Tree was kind. He gave a supper in his big room at the top of His Majesty's Theatre to which he invited many people of the theatre and many connected with the arts and social and political life. Mr. Asquith took me in to supper, and generally the evening was suggestive of generous encouragement and appreciation for the American adventurers. Mr. Sothern said a few words in which he claimed victory for our engagement, since we had lost only fifteen thousand dollars when we might quite reasonably have lost forty thousand, a quaint point of view which required some arithmetic to figure out.

The Sunken Bell puzzled the public and annoyed the reviewers. We made a mistake in opening with it. It would have been better if we had had more faith in ourselves and in Shakespeare and had opened in *Twelfth Night* or in one of our other Shakespeare plays. But we had thought it wise not to begin by facing comparisons.

The English critics did not like the *Bell* at all. I think we gave about two performances of it, then produced *Jeanne d'Arc*. That met with some favor. *Knighthood* was denounced as not of much account. But when we played *Twelfth Night* we came into our own. "Why didn't you begin with this?" asked those who wished us well. We gave our reasons but they were ineffectual; our judgment was at fault. *Romeo and Juliet* was well received as was *As You Like It*, and *Hamlet* was a decided success. Toward the end of our six weeks our houses grew, and we wound up with audiences of respectable dimensions.

One of the great delights of playing permanently in London must be the royal tribute audiences pay to actors who have served them well. I have been in a theatre on a first night when Ellen Terry and Mr. Bancroft and Marion Terry and Forbes Robertson entered the stalls, and the entire house, pit and gallery and dress circle and stalls, stood up, applauded and cheered each favorite. It is true that English audiences can be harsh, too. I have seen a wretched author called in front of the curtain that he might be "booed," and I have seen a good actor hissed.

London audiences showed us some favor and appreciation. I rather wish I could have established myself more firmly in their hearts earlier in my theatre life.

I have mentioned the highly valued opinions which made our London tour seem worth while. None was more treasured than that of the noted British critic and author, Arthur Symons.* For quoting it here I hope I may be forgiven, since it is part of the record of my life. It is glowing testimony that in the eyes of one judge I had not striven to develop my art in vain.

---

* Mr. Symons's critique under the title, "Great Acting in English," appeared in an English review soon after Miss Marlowe and Mr. Sothern had left England. It was later reprinted in a booklet and then included in his volume, *Plays, Acting, and Music*, published by E. P. Dutton & Co., New York.

It is in the staging and acting, the whole performance and management of such typical plays of Shakespeare as *Hamlet*, *Romeo and Juliet*, and *Twelfth Night* that Mr. Sothern and Miss Marlowe have shown the whole extent of their powers, and have read us the lesson we most needed. The mission of these two guests has been to show us what we have lost on our stage and what we have forgotten in our Shakespeare. And first of all I would note the extraordinary novelty and life they give to each play as a whole by their way of setting it in action. I have always felt that a play of Shakespeare, seen on the stage, should give one the same kind of impression as when one is assisting at a 'Solemn Music.' The rhythm of Shakespeare's art is not fundamentally different from that of Beethoven, and *Romeo and Juliet* is a suite, *Hamlet* a symphony. To act either of these plays with whatever qualities of another kind, and to fail in producing this musical rhythm from beginning to end is to fail in the very foundation. Here the music was unflawed; there were no depressions, no eccentricities; no sacrifice to the actor. This astonishing thing occurred; that a play was presented for its own sake, with reverence, not with ostentation; for Shakespeare's sake, not for the actor-manager's.

And from this intelligent, unostentatious way of giving Shakespeare there come to us, naturally, many lessons. Until I saw this performance of *Romeo and Juliet* I thought there was rhetoric in the play as well as the natural poetry of drama. But I see that it only needs to be acted with genius and intelligence and the poetry consumes the rhetoric. I never knew before that his play was so near to life, or that every beauty in it could be made so inevitably human. And this is because no one else has rendered, with so deep a truth, with so beautiful a fidelity, all that is passionate and desperate, and an ecstatic agony in this tragic love which glorifies and destroys Juliet. The decorative Juliet of the stage we know, the lovely picture, the ingénue, the prattler of pretty phrases, but this mysterious, tragic child whom love has made wise in making her a woman is unknown to us outside Shakespeare, and perhaps even there. Mr. Sothern's Romeo has an exquisite passion, young and extravagant as a lover's and as alive. But Miss Marlowe is not only lovely and pathetic as Juliet, she *is* Juliet. I would not say that Mr. Sothern's Hamlet is the only Hamlet, for there are still, no doubt, "points in Hamlet's soul unseized by the Germans yet." Yet what a Hamlet! How majestical, how simple, how much a poet and a gentleman! To what depth he suffers! How magnificently he interprets, in the crucifixion of his own soul, the main riddles of the universe! In *Hamlet* too I saw deeper meanings than I had ever seen in the play when it was acted. Mr. Sothern was the only quite sane Hamlet. His madness is all the outer covering of wisdom. There was nothing fantastic in his grave, subdued, powerful and piteous representation, in which no symbol, no metaphysical Faust, no figment of a German brain loomed before us, but a man more to be pitied and not less to be honoured than any man in Elsinore. I have seen romantic, tragic, exceptional Hamlets, the very bells on the cap of "Fortune's fool." But at last I have seen the man himself—as Shakespeare saw him living. A gentleman as well as a philosopher, a nature of fundamental sincerity; no melancholy clown, but the greatest of all critics of life. And the play with its melodrama and its lyrical ecstasy moved before one's eyes like a religious service.

How is it that we get from the acting and management of these two actors a result which no one in England has ever been able to get? Well, in the first place, as I have said, they have the odd caprice of preferring Shakespeare to themselves; the odd conviction that fidelity to Shakespeare will give them the best chance of doing great things themselves. Nothing is accidental. Everything obeys a single intention. Now here are two players in whom technique has been carried to a supreme point. There is no actor on our stage who can speak either English or verse as these two Americans can. It is on this preliminary technique, the power of using speech as one uses the notes of a musical instrument that all possibility of great acting depends. Who is there that can give us not the external gesture but the inner meaning of some beautiful and subtle passage of Shakespeare? One of our great actors will give it sonorously, as rhetoric, and another eagerly as passionate speech, but no one with the precise accent of a man who is speaking his thoughts, which is what Shakespeare makes his characters do when he puts his loveliest poetry into their mouths. Look at Mr. Sothern when he gives the soliloquy "To be, or not to be" which we are accustomed to hear spoken to the public in one or another of many rhetorical manners. Mr. Sothern's Hamlet curls himself up on a chair exactly as sensitive, reflective people do when they want to make their bodies comfortable before setting their minds to work; and he lets you overhear his thoughts. Every soliloquy of Shakespeare is meant to be over-

heard and just so casually to render this on the stage requires
first an understanding of what poetry is—next a perfect capacity of producing by the sound and intonation of the voice
the exact meaning of those words and cadences. Who is there
on our stage who has completely mastered those two first requirements of acting? No one now acting in English except
Julia Marlowe and Edward Sothern.

What these two players do is to give us not the impression
which we get when we see and admire fine limitations, but
the impression which we get from real people who when they
speak in verse seem to be speaking merely the language of
their own hearts. They give us every character in the round,
whereas with our actors we see no more than profiles. Look
for contrast at the Malvolio of Mr. Sothern. It is an elaborate travesty done in a disguise like solemn dandy's head of
Disraeli. He acts with his eyelids, which move while all
the rest of his face is motionless; with his pursed, reticent
mouth, with his prim and pompous gestures, with that self-
consciousness which brings all Malvolio's troubles upon him.
It is a fantastic, tragically comic thing, done with rare cal-
culation, and it has its formal, almost cruel share in the immense gaiety of the piece. The play is great and wild, a mockery and a happiness; and it is all seen and not interpreted,
but the mystery of it deepened in the clown's song at the
end, which for once has been allowed its full effect, not theatrical, but of pure imagination.

So far I have spoken only of those first requirements, those
elementary principles of acting which we ought to be able to
take for granted; only, in England, we cannot. These once

granted, the individual work of the actor begins, his power to create with the means at his disposal. Let us look then a little more closely at Miss Marlowe. I have spoken of her Juliet which is no doubt her finest part. But now look at her Ophelia. It is not perhaps so great a triumph as her Juliet, and merely for the reason that there is little in Ophelia but an image of some beautiful bright thing broken. Yet the mad scene will be remembered among all other renderings for its edged lightness, the quite simple poetry it makes of madness —above all the natural pity that comes into it from a complete abandonment to what is essence and not mere decoration, in the spoiled brain of this kind, loving and will-less woman. She suffers and is pitifully unaware of it, there before you, the very soul naked and shameless with an innocence beyond innocence. She makes the rage and tenderness of Hamlet towards her a credible thing.

In Juliet, Miss Marlowe is ripe humanity, in Ophelia that same humanity broken down from within. As Viola in *Twelfth Night* she is the woman let loose to be bewitching in spite of herself. And here again her art is tested and triumphs, for she is bewitching and never trespasses into jauntiness on the one hand or, on the other, into that modern sentiment which the theatre has accustomed itself to under the name of Romance. She is serious, with a calm and even simplicity to which everything is a kind of child's play, putting no unnecessary pathos into a matter destined to become right in the end. And so her delicate and unrestrained gaiety in masquerade interprets perfectly, satisfies every requirement of what for the moment is whimsical in Shakespeare's art. . . .

Duse is the soul made flesh, Réjane the flesh made Parisian, Sarah Bernhardt the flesh and the devil; but Julia Marlowe is the joy of life, the plenitude of sap in the tree.

During my stay in London I received a letter from Signor D'Annunzio, whose play, *Francesca da Rimini*, I had proposed to produce in America. Madame Duse had used her good offices in my favor. He sent me a very beautiful vellum-covered copy of his play and a photograph inscribed *"a la Divine Julia Marlowe."* This custom of addressing the distinguished artiste as divine is a pretty one which we will be slow to embrace in our democracy although the French have not neglected so bright a compliment to La Divine Sarah, nor the Italians to La Divine Duse. I felt flattered to be among the goddesses.

On the conclusion of our London engagement we returned to New York and played our repertoire at the Academy of Music to great audiences, speedily recouping the expenses of our English experiment. Our agent had a huge electric sign placed over the front of the theatre in which burning letters spelled the legend, "Welcome Home." One of the New York papers with no respect for divinities proclaimed that there could be no question of the sincerity of the sentiment since we had paid for it ourselves. Be that as it may, our season progressed to its conclusion with excellent results, and the third year of Mr. Sothern's association with me had fulfilled all that I had hoped from it. We had benefited both professionally and financially, and I felt that our combination had won golden opinions from all sorts of people.

chapter 17

Ring Out the New

When our dual star agreement expired, it seemed wise to Mr. Sothern and me to follow separate paths again for a while. Since I did not wish to begin by repeating alone dramas we had played together—that would be risking a loss of public interest—I searched for a new play.

My choice was *Gloria* by James B. Fagan, a romantic comedy, its scene laid in Italy during the Renaissance. It provided me with a good comedy part and was received with satisfaction by my clientele. Later I played *Romeo and Juliet* with Frederic Lewis as Romeo through a profitable season.

Opening a new play had been a business necessity, for we who deal in entertainment must have the benefit of advertising, and it is novelty that provokes discussion. The narrow path of a devotion to Shakespeare could be traveled only under such circumstances as I had enjoyed during the past three years. A broader road must be accepted now.

The next year I produced a play by Miss Mary Johnstone,* *The Goddess of Reason*, a story of the French Revolution. It was an ambitious drama, written in verse and requiring a cast of fifty characters along with large assemblies: mobs, soldiers and so on. William Winter and some of my more severe critics expressed only qualified approval but confessed that it was powerful theatrically and that Miss Johnstone had provided me

* American historical novelist, author of *To Have and To Hold*.

with a role which gave me many fine opportunities. I continued in that drama for the entire season and found a gratifying reception wherever I went.

In 1909 was launched a public-spirited project, the New Theatre of New York. J. P. Morgan, W. K. Vanderbilt, Clarence Mackay and other wealthy men contributed generously. The venture was housed in a splendid building at Sixtieth Street and Central Park West which stood until 1931 as its monument. I was offered a position in the enterprise, and Mr. Sothern was also approached. Naturally we both were interested in any movement for the betterment and dignity of the theatre. The prospect of being able to forward in any way the purpose which the founders had in view filled us with an eager desire to aid in any way we could.

Soon we agreed with the management of the new enterprise that we should each of us abandon private ventures and throw in our fortunes with the New Theatre for a period of three years. Here lay a great opportunity of providing New York with an institution similar to the House of Molière in Paris, conducted on the policy of the great Continental municipal and government playhouses.

The policy as first announced was to combine opera and drama. I am aware that in the case of the "Old Vic" in London that procedure was successfully accomplished, but I venture to think it was a fundamental error in the case of the New Theatre. Also it was decided to enter into competition with the regular theatre managers by the production of new plays. That in itself was a not unreasonable intention had the new play been selected with the discreet deliberation which would seem to be essential to the growth of really fine dramas. The experienced managers of the great foreign theatres find it possible to produce an excellent new play now and then, but it is difficult, I imagine, to secure one very good new play of the higher class, let alone a number within a short period. On the other hand our English drama is rich in comedy and tragedy of the highest quality: not alone Shakespeare but Sheridan, Goldsmith, Ben Jonson, and some of the Restoration dramatists reasonably edited. A list of moderns such as Pinero, Henry Arthur Jones, Sir James Barrie and some of our American authors would have provided a rich repertoire which, with a frequent change of bill, would have kept fine drama before the public.

The New Theatre had its beautiful building, but the essence of such an enterprise is no more bricks and mortar than with a public library or national museum. Mr. Sothern and I had been paid the high compliment of being chosen to star in the first production. Yet not two but a company of well-trained actors was an essential, and such a company should have been established before the erection of the building. When those actors, endowed with a rich repertoire, had, through experience, experiment, and elimination, evolved into as fine and as accomplished a band of players as could possibly be gathered together, then they should have been housed in their theatre and have produced their repertoire.

That is actually what happened in the case of Molière's company, although the greater part of his plays were written after he had found royal favor. A modern instance is the New York Theatre Guild, which, having won the confidence and the esteem of the public, has been rewarded by subscriptions which enabled it to build its own home.

Circumstances arose which made it advisable for Mr. Sothern and myself to resign from the New Theatre effective when we completed our engagement in *Antony and Cleopatra.** We believed it to be to the best interest of the enterprise that we go.

After about three months we arranged to gather most of our old associates and opened at the Academy of Music with a repertoire of six of Shakespeare's plays: *As You Like It, Romeo and Juliet, Hamlet, The Taming of the Shrew, Twelfth Night* and *The Merchant of Venice.* Our reunion was greeted with enthusiasm by our friends, and we continued throughout the season to play to excellent houses all over the country.

Later when the New Theatre had been rechristened The Century, we played a remarkable engagement there to receipts of over twenty-five thousand dollars a week, the great stage giving us scope for fine productions of all our plays. It was on this occasion that we gave a free matinee performance for school children and had the delightful experience of having as our guests five thousand little folk who sat silent and enthralled throughout the tragedy of *Hamlet.* We had selected it because of the charge that Shakespeare is highbrow, although the playwright himself was at pains to call attention to the fact that the groundlings attended his performances to such an extent as to be troublesome. Groundlings, however, were an indispensable part of the audience in the days of Queen Elizabeth, and plays

---

* Neither Miss Marlowe nor Mr. Sothern would have selected *Antony and Cleopatra* of their own accord. It was chosen by the New Theatre as in the nature of a novelty, a Shakespearean play in which neither of the two noted Shakespearean actors had previously appeared. There were difficulties with the theatre's stage manager, imported from England. The stars played out the twelve weeks for which seats had been subscribed, then severed all connections with the enterprise.

This episode is quite fully related in Russell's biography, pp. 465–75—"The New Theatre Disasters." Evidently the whole affair was so distressing to Miss Marlowe and to Mr. Sothern that the latter avoided going into it in detail.

had to contain such ingredients as would attract them. Such ingredients *Hamlet* had and has—it would engage the attention of a deaf man. The action is constant and exciting and accelerates in interest until the very end. Our five thousand little children perceived nothing highbrow about the play, and their silence and their applause was governed by as great an understanding as adults'.

In Chicago, also, we gave a free performance for school children, playing *The Merchant of Venice* to a crowded house. The youngsters, who had just taken part in open-air exhibitions, marched through the streets to the theatre in their costumes. They showed great enthusiasm and an intelligence not unworthy of a grown-up audience. At the end of the trial scene, there were many calls, and one small auditor stood on the railing of a private box and shouted, "Gee! This beats the nickel show!"

That struck us as an excellent Shakespearean commentary— one at which the poet himself would have rejoiced.

The following year we played *Twelfth Night* in Chicago at a children's matinee to a similar happy reception. Had we been able to continue in the theatre, we intended to make occasional free performances for children a part of our regular schedule. Not only was it a joy to give pleasure to the children, but the shows were a sound business proposition. We believed that in planting the seed early we would reap a crop of theatregoers later on among those who might never have come in contact with such plays except through such an opportunity.

One day when Mr. Sothern and I were filling an engagement in Kansas City, we were invited to go to a high school to speak to the pupils. We accepted gladly, and in the large auditorium, jammed with students large and small, Mr. Sothern gave a talk about the theatre. When he felt that attention was wandering, he said, "I don't want to bother you with talk about the theatre if you are not much interested. How would you like me to read to you? Shall I recite something?" A great shout arose, "Recite, recite!" Mr. Sothern read several scenes from *Hamlet* and other plays, along with some poems. Then he urged that I should recite, which I did. All was now alertness and enthusiasm.

"I see what you want is a show," said Mr. Sothern. When we vitalized the words with skillful reading and impersonation, the children could see the persons of the drama. As a result they sought out the plays we had read from and began to study them with a new interest. On the Saturday afternoon of our Kansas City engagement, as Mr. Sothern came out of the stage door, one of the schoolmasters greeted him with, "You will, I am sure, be interested to know that after you and Miss Marlowe had read to our boys and girls, three hundred of them secured seats for this matinee and have been here to-day."

It is not only in such trial scenes as that of *The Merchant of Venice* that we of the theatre must have to do with the law. Readers will remember how I won a suit in Indianapolis against a critic who libeled my company.

While I was still playing at the New Theatre in New York, I had an unpleasant, inexplicable experience with a guardian of the law. As I was hurrying from the Plaza Hotel across the Park to my matinee, I lost my bearings and could not be sure as to the exact location of that exit from the park nearest to the theatre. I asked a big park policeman to direct me. To my horror and indignation he hit me a whack on the back and said,

"Go along with ye! A fine girl like you to lose your way! There ye are now. Off you go," and he whacked me again. I left him with much dignity, and in a moment I discovered that my nose was bleeding profusely. He had hit me so hard that I was shedding blood copiously and had to make my way in this gory state through the streets to my dressing room, and was much delayed in my preparations for the stage. That Egypt's Queen should suffer such indignity! I really wished that I were for one moment Cleopatra that I might persuade that Irishman it was folly to treat royal personages with such familiarity. Probably he would have said that he was himself a king.

Also at that time Mr. Sothern and I were sued by two Boston writers from whom we had obtained a translation of Gabriele D'Annunzio's play, *The Daughter of Jorio*. We had prepared the scenery, costumes and properties for an elaborate production and put it into rehearsal. When we began to read the lines, however, we discovered grave defects we had previously missed. Since Arthur Symons of London had made another version of the play, we endeavored to make arrangements with the Boston authors for a release. We were not able to reach a settlement, so we decided we would not produce the play. An action was then taken and came into court in New York. Our counsel pleaded that had we produced the version we considered so unworthy we would have had to withdraw it. Here was a delicate question. The judge, however, was a Solomon. He solved the matter by asking me if I would read a passage aloud from the Symons' version and the same passage from that of the Boston writers. I did so, trying to do justice to each. The judge took the case from the jury and gave a decision in our favor.

chapter 18

"Drum and Colours"

We produced the tragedy of *Macbeth* in the season of 1910–11. I had played Cleopatra at the New Theatre, but Lady Macbeth was the first tragic role I had assumed under our own management, with the conduct of the entire play under our control. The production met with great praise; along with the other plays on our list it constituted a repertoire of eight Shakespearean dramas with which we toured the country. Mr. Sothern also played *If I Were King* at the Wednesday matinees and thus enabled me to confine my own labors to seven performances a week.

Nine heavy productions necessitated a serious outlay. We required a train of six baggage cars for the scenery and four other cars, including a private one. Public response, however, was so generous that the enterprise was in every way successful.

While in California we gave a performance of *Macbeth* in the great open-air theatre at Berkeley, a difficult matter, for the play is in many scenes. But we arranged a set of powerful electric lights, put on at the end of a scene, and they served the purpose of a curtain since the blaze of light obscured the view of the stage. Thus we were enabled to change our properties unseen by the audience. Distances from one side of the stage to the other were so great that our players were constantly sprinting to get here or there on time and would often arrive breathless for their entrance.

A remarkable natural effect was created in the first scene with the witches. A mist came up from the sea just as the scene was about to begin and shrouded the stage, so that when the weird sisters chanted:

> Fair is foul and foul is fair.
> Hover through the fog and filthy air.

the effect was realistic to a degree—awful and mysterious. The mist rolled over the stage and faded away just as the next scene began. Excellent celestial stage management!

At the conclusion of the season Mr. Sothern and I were married in London on August 11, 1911.*

We had gone abroad in company with a close friend, a German physician who went to Berlin for some weeks and rejoined us in London. We told him that we contemplated the purchase of a house in the neighborhood of Stratford-on-Avon. He became very much disturbed and begged of us on no account to invest our money in any such venture. He declared that there would be war between England and Germany soon and that the result was inevitable: England would without question be defeated. Said he, "You don't want to buy a house in a conquered country." He said he had talked with persons who were in a position to know, and that there could be no doubt whatever as to the truth of his information.

Nevertheless we continued house-hunting in England, and it occasioned some amusing experiences. The English are proud

---

* "Their artistic and business partnership had been led in the most complete harmony; their tastes, ideas, and ambitions were in all ways the same; and their friends felt that here was a union uncommonly auspicious and happy."—C. E. Russell

of their ancient buildings and restore them with much enthusiasm, so it is quite usual to read advertisements which en-
tice the would-be purchaser with flowery and pleasant descrip-
tions of old priories, abbeys, castles and so forth. A great many
of them are genuine enough, but they also are in many instances
mere shells of what they once were, having been half destroyed
during one or another of the various civil wars. The induce-
ment usually adopted is to declare that such crippled relics are
"easily added to"—which indeed is quite true—but the addi-
tions themselves may prove to be exceedingly elaborate, and
in many cases only a few old Tudor bricks or stones remain of
the original structure. With a gay heart the house-hunter journeys to distant parts of the country, only to discover that the
coveted priory consists of little but the foundations.

The American is at once recognized by the house agent.
There is something about the cut of his jib which reveals him
instantly. I myself was born in England, and Mr. Sothern was
brought up and at school there until he was about nineteen. I
do not think that either of us has an American accent. Yet even
when dressed entirely in English clothes—hatted, habited,
haberdashed, booted, barbered and walking-sticked by English
tradesmen—the estate man would spot us at once and begin to
play upon our supposed American proclivity for seeking the
ancient and historically curious. Mr. Sothern has a fancy for
moated granges, and we had become enamored of such lovely
places as Compton Wyneates and Eightam Mote, and had run
about all over England seeking such picturesque houses.

One day we visited a London agent who in a moment
scented our nationality. "Oh, yes," said he, "we have a great
many American gentlemen who want houses of that class. I

know just what you want. You'd like a place with a moat or perhaps an old Tudor house where Queen Elizabeth slept. Yes, yes, quite so. Or a Jacobean house, one where King Charles hid before the Battle of Worcester. One of those places with the priests' hole—I know—I know—exactly—quite—quite—a secret passage perhaps. They come along now and then." He began to turn over the leaves of a ledger. "Let me see—moats— no—I don't think we can suit you there. No—we have no moats; a ghost, perhaps—we frequently have them. Haunted— a place with some historical interest—some mystery maybe. No—no—we have no place like that." He turned more pages. "No place where Queen Elizabeth slept—no priests' hole—no secret passage. Here we are. Here's a splendid place with a curse on it."

The splendid place with the curse looked rather like a ruined cow-house in a photograph which he produced, so we were not beguiled.

We made an excursion, however, to a house some hours from London. An old lady with much manner conducted us for a considerable distance over many fields and at last pointed to the remains, grass-grown and scanty, of what once, no doubt, had been a human habitation. One wall was standing, in it a Gothic window. "An old priory," she declared with awe. "Very old indeed. Just look through this window. You can actually see the monks as they sat at the long refectory table. On the other side there was the solar chamber, and no doubt the prior looked through one of those spy places in the wall to see what his monks were doing. Of course, the place could be rebuilt— one could do anything one likes with it—reconstruct the whole building. I think that's so much better than having it all ready to move into. It isn't your house then, it's somebody else's house."

"But," said Mr. Sothern, "it isn't a house at all. There's nothing but this one window."

"Of course," agreed the lady. "That's just it. It's a ruin. That's where the romance is. Don't you love it?"

But we could not summon up any affection, and as we walked back to the village where our guide resided, a sort of gloom settled on the conversational effort. She assumed an air of mystery. She stood still in the middle of a field, looked about her and put her finger to her lips. "I must tell you," said she, "I must tell you they *do* say there's a buried treasure here." And she nodded with an air of secrecy and much significance.

But the place struck us as hardly a safe investment, so we let it slip and maybe lost a fortune.

In the charming city of Worcester we visited the Commandry, a delightful building of many interesting associations now occupied by a publishing concern. A particularly English old gentleman took great delight in showing us over the house, which was beautifully paneled in every chamber. The bedrooms contained wonderful, carved four-post beds of black oak and excellent collections of chairs and silver. Our conductor spotted us at once as inquisitive Americans and became extremely garrulous. "I had an American gentleman here the other day," said he. "Quaint, very quaint. Your people speak right out from the shoulder—say what they mean. No beating about the bush. A word and a blow, as it were—quick—to the point. I showed this countryman of yours over the place—opened his eyes, I can tell you. What do you think he said, now? What do you think he said?"

We confessed we were unable to imagine. "Of course you can't," he babbled. "Who could? Why, he stood here looking at this very bed, and he waved his arm as if to take in the whole house and everything in it, myself included. 'What will you take for the whole shootin' match?' he asked."

It sounded something like one of our acquisitive explorers —and I wondered whether the "shootin' match" man were a moving picture magnate or maybe one of the gentlemen of the prize ring. He certainly could not have been a Shakespearean actor.

We gave up our search for a relic of the English past. Home we went—and found ourselves occupying a series of modern American houses.

During the next theatrical season we introduced a novel plan into our scheme of living. I was not well when we reached St. Louis, and the doctors recommended a food regimen, impossible to observe in hotels. Mr. Sothern inquired as to the chance of securing a furnished house for the one week of our engagement. House agents regarded such a request as sheer madness. A furnished house for one week! However, he did persuade some people who lived near the park to rent us their nice flat for a week, and he went to an employment bureau and engaged two servants. As it happened they were both good cooks, although one was willing to do the housework. The plan succeeded to perfection, and we engaged them permanently to travel with us, and in advance we secured houses in all the cities we played in, even when we appeared for only three nights. The comfort of such a way of living, especially for a woman, quite revolutionized the wandering life to which I had so long been accustomed. All the home-longing which wearies the spirit was banished. We would usually reach our new city on a Sunday and drive at once to some charming house on the outskirts of the town. There would be established one of our two cooks who had left the last city on Friday, done her marketing on Saturday, and had our dinner ready for us on Sunday night. Usually we secured beautiful houses, standing in their own grounds. The advent of the automobile had created very pleasant suburbs outside most of the cities, and in Cincinnati, Pittsburgh, St. Louis and Cleveland, which used to be sombre places to visit, we occupied charming homes. The actual expense of such a manner of living was not in the end much more extravagant than the best hotels.

Nevertheless ten weeks after we had started our season I was seized with an illness in Los Angeles and had to stop work. I went to New York and suffered from a serious breakdown which utterly incapacitated me for some months. Mr. Sothern reorganized our company, discarded our Shakespeare repertoire which he knew would not draw houses without me—a penalty for such associations. He continued to play *Hamlet* but added his father's play, *Lord Dundreary*, *If I Were King*, and *Richard Lovelace* by Laurence Irving. When he reached Chicago, he produced a new play by Justin McCarthy, *Charlemagne*. It was an elaborate production, but it did not meet with success and has not been played outside of Chicago.

The outbreak of the Great War of 1914 caught us in London. I had secured accommodation at Franzenbad, where I intended to undergo the cure, and was about to start when the Serbian note set the world ablaze. Mr. Sothern concluded that I had better return to Litchfield, Connecticut, where we had previously spent the summer, and we sailed on the *Mauretania* on July twenty-ninth. On the fourth of August when we went down to dinner, we found all the portholes were covered by canvas. This, of course, excited comment but rough weather was predicted. At about twelve o'clock that night Mr. Sothern was pacing the deck outside our room; the full moon was bright in the sky and shone immediately over the stern of the ship. Of a sudden the ship slowed down, then turned at an acute angle, the moon now being at the right. Then the vessel seemed to slip a leash and trembled as it rushed through the sea. We were bound for Halifax. England had entered the war. German warships were on the watch for the *Mauretania*, and the *Emden* was known to be close at hand. But we reached port safely and as we entered the harbor a British gunboat passed us, her colors flying, the band playing *Rule, Britannia*, and the bluejackets cheering.

A personal tragedy was in store for us. While spending the spring in Washington, we heard the news of the sinking of the *Lusitania*, and the death of Charles Frohman, our old-time manager and friend. Mr. Sothern and I had been to New York just previous to his sailing and had called on him, for he had been very ill. He was still suffering and was crippled by his sickness but as ever he was cheerful and full of fun. For half an hour he joked and laughed and after we went away he sent a letter to say he was sailing on the *Lusitania*, and urging us to go with him. Indeed we seriously thought of doing so but providentially postponed our trip.

In 1915, George Washington University conferred on Mr. Sothern the honorary degree of Doctor of Letters in recognition of his services to the American Theatre, a distinction which gave us both gratification.

That same year we attended the Frances Scott Key Celebration at Baltimore, where I had the pleasure of reciting the *Star-Spangled Banner* in the armory before some thousands of people. That poem has been somewhat severely criticized as a work of art, but it has some qualities which, apart from the sentiment of the occasion, permits of stirring delivery by one able to perceive its possibilities. So its reception by the audience proved. The Mayor of Baltimore presented me with a commemoration medal and a gold casket containing a parchment granting the freedom of the city.

The following season, 1915–16, Mr. Sothern undertook to act alone. He produced *The Two Virtues* by Alfred Sutro at the Boston Theatre in New York with Miss Haidee Wright in a leading part. After a considerable run he put on *Lord Dundreary* again and later Robertson's *David Garrick*. Then he finished the season with a tour. I joined him in Toronto, and there he and I and Miss Wright and the other members of the company worked for the recruiting service. We gave a benefit performance, and in the streets and in front of the Court House gave recitations under the auspices of the Commander of the "Buffs," a regiment which later distinguished itself at the front.

At the end of this year I announced my retirement from the stage and at the time was entirely sincere in my wish to be relieved from my exhausting work in the theatre. My late illness had greatly taxed my strength, and Mr. Sothern felt he did not care to continue since he would have to abandon our plays which we had built up in public favor together. Our announcement brought forth delightful evidences of generous regret, which took the form of public banquets, among them one given by the Twilight Club, one by the Civic Forum, and one by the Society of Arts and Sciences. On the latter occasion Dr. John Finley, on behalf of the Society, presented Mr. Sothern with its medal for distinguished services to Art and Letters. The invitation to the dinner tendered by the Civic Forum I must reproduce, for I am very proud of it.

New York, January Twenty-first, 1916

To Mr. and Mrs. Edward H. Sothern.

For many years, with a genius and devotion worthy of the highest admiration, you have both rendered inestimable service to dramatic art in this country and particularly to the production of Shakespearean drama. It is not possible to express to you adequately the appreciation of your work felt by a multitude of your countrymen but we desire deeply to make such recognition of it and of our regard for you as it is in our power to make. We therefore, the undersigned, on our own behalf and on behalf of many others, take the greatest pleasure in inviting you to accept a testimonial Banquet in your honor to take place in this city on a date convenient to yourselves within the near future. It would seem to us particularly fortunate if this date were to be about the time of the observance of the Shakespeare Tercentenary in April.

(Signed)

Joseph H. Choate
Robert Underwood Johnson
Kate Douglas Wiggin
Brander Mathews
Henry W. Taft
Winthrop Ames
Cass Gilbert
Augustus Thomas
Robert Erskine Ely
Henry Clews
Walter Damrosch
Hamilton Wright Mabie
Otto H. Kahn
George McAnerny
Daniel C. French
A. Barton Hepburn
Talcott Williams
Paul D. Cravath
Isaac M. Seligman
Hamilton Holt
Edwin H. Blashfield
Marcus M. Marks.

Robert Underwood Johnson read a poem for the occasion, and Theodore Roosevelt's sister, Mrs. Corinne Roosevelt Robinson, rendered the following amusing tribute:

Flanked by such comrades, I am loath to lift
A trembling voice as one who is the rift
Within the lute. For how can I aspire
To rival all the past and future fire
Of incense burned before this gifted pair—
Sothern and Marlowe—two beyond compare.

August is Thomas, waiting at my side,
To prove that words and wit are fast allied
And if he can't suffice in his short span
To stir the house to homage—Otto *Kahn!*

And Agnes Repplier, she of rapier blade,
Has cast all other speakers in the shade
Except that one whose method no one shames,
So nobly conscious is he of his *Ames!*

Now mark 'em all, yes, Edwin Markham too—
To think that I should follow one like you—
Poet and prophet, master of the flow
That makes a hero wield for sword a hoe!
So listen, friends, with kind and lenient ear,
To these few lines that I would have you hear—
Lines only worth your favor since they dwell
On two we honor—two we love so well.

First to the man—though ladies should be first—
Who but remembers how he slaked our thirst
For high Romance—when tried and true and tender
He made us all believe there was a Zenda?
Or who forgets his gay and debonair,
Inimitable laughing Lettarblair?
And Chumley—echoed from a brilliant sire—
The memory of hours that could not tire?
Magnetic magic joined to all that's human;
Of course he knew "the way to win a woman."

And so he won her—she who had already
Inflamed our brains and made our hearts unsteady—
Who by the wonder of her low, deep voice
Could make an audience tremble or rejoice,
Whose *Barbara Frietchie* thrilled us over much
(Methinks she'd sensed e'en then the *Southern* touch).
She who with dainty grace and poignant power
Had made us live *When Knighthood Was in Flower*.

He won her and as one they climbed the height
Of Shakespeare's "jocund morn" or "dreadful night."
And we who enter now a holy place

Would bend with reverend knee, though lifted face,
Before the fair presentments they have made.
Here is our tribute. May it then be laid
With loving ardor at the altar-throne
Of two who made great Shakespeare all their own—
This "wise young judge," this madcap Rosalind,
Gay shrew untamed and yet not half unkind,
Fair Juliet, so bewitching her caress
Had left sweet Romeo in a sorry stress—
Or Viola, part boy yet wholly woman,
Capricious, tender, petulant and human.
And now in turn behold as in a glass
The fawning Shylock or Malvolio pass,
Or suddenly with quick vibrating pain
We sense the torture of the noble Dane—
Or yield ourselves, philosophers as well,
To melancholy Jaques' potent spell—

We crown them with their vast achievement. Rise
And honor those who read the mysteries
Of Avon's Bard, and read them all aright.
Who would not then be Julia's satellite
Or Sothern's slave? Once more the laurel bring
To her, the queen of queens, "If he were king."

Later on we were presented with a beautiful illuminated
volume, vellum-covered, which contained the addresses of the
evening and the signatures of officials and guests.

About this time Robert Bridges, of *Scribner's Magazine*,
which had published some chapters of Mr. Sothern's book,

The Melancholy Tale of Me, told us that Theodore Roosevelt
had been so entertained by them that he wanted us both to
lunch with him at Oyster Bay. Of course we went, and a fine
time we had. Mr. and Mrs. Roosevelt were charming, and we
drank in many tales of Colonel Roosevelt's adventures.

In 1916–17 Mr. Sothern made a contract to appear in moving pictures for the Vitagraph Company at Coney Island. Unfortunately the pictures were not a great success. Two modern
plays which were written for Mr. Sothern did not exhibit him
in the environment to which his audiences had become accustomed. But the third picture, a version of the play, *An
Enemy to the King*, was more appealing and in that he appeared to advantage.

When the three pictures were finished, Mr. Sothern, feeling that his days of active work in the theatre were numbered,
offered through Daniel Frohman to donate to the Actors Fund
of America the proceeds of a two weeks' engagement in New
York. The proposal was accepted and fourteen performances
of Justin McCarthy's play *If I Were King*, were given at the
Shubert Theatre. At that time I took a formal farewell in the
shape of a special performance for the French wounded. There
were currently many other benefits for the war sufferers which
kept theatrical people busy. On various occasions at the Cana-
dian Club at the Hotel Biltmore we took a willing part.

At length Mr. Sothern felt so strongly the impulse to aid the
Red Cross that he determined to devote an entire season to the
cause. He gathered his forces together and started on a tour
with *If I Were King*. Lee Shubert agreed to give twenty-five
per cent of every performance to the Red Cross, and more than

twenty-five thousand dollars were sent abroad to England. Then suddenly Mr. Sothern was stricken down and for thirteen weeks was confined to his bed in New York.

At last, in 1917, the United States entered the war. We, among many actors, took part in drives for the armed forces. We went to the old Stewart Store at Park Street and to other places to address great gatherings, and when the Liberty Loan operations were started, with many hundreds of our people, we took part in the appeals from the rostrum in front of the Public Library, in the Biltmore Hotel, and at the Waldorf where I stood on tables to read and recite.

In February, Mr. Sothern went to France with Winthrop Ames to learn what help actors could render the troops now pouring into the great conflict. They and Mrs. Ames traveled all over the American front. They visited General Pershing's headquarters at Chaumont and discussed with him the ways and means of contributing the most effective service. Under the auspices of the Y.M.C.A. they were permitted to penetrate so far to the front that they could hear the great guns and at night see the flash of their fire near at hand.

Soon hundreds of small parties of entertainers under the auspices of the Y.M.C.A. would be organized to follow their route and with music and little plays do what they might to relieve the dreadful strain and monotony of the soldier's life. They went to many of the Y.M.C.A. huts, and my husband joined in the entertainments then being given by the men themselves, trying to learn by experience what sort of thing they liked.

One night at an entertainment, Mr. Sothern was reading

the closet scene from *Hamlet* where the Prince rebukes his mother for her marriage with his uncle. He had just reached that moment when Hamlet stabs the eavesdropping Polonius behind the curtain and had uttered the Queen's line, "Oh, what a rash and bloody deed is this," when there was a dreadful crash outside the hut. "Lights out!" cried a voice, and the electric switches were turned off. An air raid was on. Bombs crashed again and again. It seemed that the hut must be annihilated. At length a bugle sounded the all clear, and lights went on. A colonel asked, "Now, Mr. Sothern, will you go on?" And again my husband spoke the line, "Oh, what a rash and bloody deed is this." A great shout of approval went up at the most appropriate words.

When Mr. Ames returned to New York, a great meeting was held at the Palace Theatre, and he and Mr. Sothern placed the facts they had gathered before the assembled men and women of the stage and asked their help on behalf of the soldiers. The response was quick, and Mr. Ames and Mr. Edward F. Albee soon started a bureau to send overseas numerous small parties which performed valiantly until long after the Armistice.

After a few weeks my husband crossed the ocean again on a ship crowded with soldiers, and for some months, under the direction of Madame Hortense Paulsen, he toured England and Scotland with various concert parties to those districts occupied by the American forces. In some remote seaport in Scotland he recited Helen Gray Cone's stirring poem, "England," which cries out for recognition of all the martial and civil qualities which have made Britain what she is, each stanza concluding with the word, "England," uttered proudly, vehemently. After the entertainment was over, a kilted Scotch soldier on crutches approached Mr. Sothern and said, "I'll tell ye, the next time ye gie that poem say 'Scotland.' Ye ken Scotland's in this war."

Miss Mary Anderson * associated herself with many of the entertainments in which Mr. Sothern took part, and they played together some scenes from *Macbeth.*

Mr. Sothern returned from England just before the Armistice, and we were in New York when the false rumor came, and the city went wild. Then came the true assurance that the war was over. There was, however, much time before American troops could be brought home, and there was still work to be done by the entertaining units. I went abroad in the service of the Y.M.C.A. and traveled over England and Scotland where Mr. Sothern and I gave many readings in clubs and huts and halls. The sort of thing we were capable of contributing we had feared would not be acceptable, but we found the troops very appreciative, and on several occasions we gave programs which by request consisted entirely of scenes and selections from Shakespeare.

On several occasions we went to Stratford-on-Avon. There Miss Marie Corelli had donated the use of a huge schoolhouse which adjoined her own residence and which she had purchased for use as an officers' club. Many Americans on leave were glad to avail themselves of the chance to visit Stratford under such pleasant conditions. We were present at the opening of

* Mary Anderson (1859–1940), an American actress of charm and beauty, made her stage debut at sixteen as Juliet. She also played many of the other roles for which Julia Marlowe later became renowned. She had retired in 1889, married and settled in England but emerged from retirement to appear in benefit performances during World War I.

this clubhouse, and a pleasant supper was given at the ceremony.

On the voyage back to New York on board the *Aquitania* there were seven thousand American soldiers. A boxing exhibition was given on one of the lower decks, with Benny Leonard, the lightweight champion, taking on various opponents. I was seated next to General Kennedy by the ringside when Mr. Leonard delivered a knockout blow, and his adversary fell with his forehead resting upon my right foot. My husband saw me change color as the fallen boxer lay still. The unconscious man was turned over, his chest heaved and shortly he was as well as ever. But I was not eager to see any more knockouts.

On our return to New York Mr. Shubert held out such attractive inducements for a season of our plays that we were easily persuaded to accept. By now the value of a dollar had been reduced to about sixty cents, and like many others who had thought they had enough to retire on and enjoy some years of repose after labor, we found that our resources were seriously depleted. Therefore we prepared for a tour with our repertoire, but all our equipment had been sold, so an entirely new outfit was needed. In view of the great expense which the reproduction of so many plays would entail, we decided to make some concession to the modern spirit which had accepted as excellent a sort of revival or adaptation of the Elizabethan stage.

Our scheme consisted of a permanent front stage, supported upon four columns, and of several sets of draperies at various distances from the footlights. All was painted in a green-gray neutral color which nevertheless exhibited variety of tone. Locality was determined by back drops and a few stage properties such as a wellhead, a stone seat, Juliet's balcony, some furniture. We gained immensely in speed and were enabled to cut down our acting time by over an hour. These backgrounds when lighted with skill were extremely beautiful and indeed were sufficient. In time possibly people would have wearied of them as people do weary of everything. But our own purpose was served. The new school of stage decoration was well illustrated, and the "progressives" exhibited some satisfaction that we of the despised Victorian Era had surrendered to the enlightened present.

Another innovation which we found to our advantage was the abolition of all incidental music save what could be properly incorporated in the action of the play. We entirely dispensed with the orchestra in front of the curtain; we had no music between the acts. Our audiences approved. Even the inadequate orchestra of former days, on account of the great expense of running a theatre, had been reduced to the proportions of the baffled brotherhood of Old King Cole, whose fiddlers three soothed the spirit of that merry old soul. But to a spirit not fortified with pipe and bowl these depleted bands produced a mood of melancholy which we felt would depress our public.

So we once more took to the "road," and during the season of 1919–20 enjoyed a phenomenal prosperity.

chapter 19

"Fair Ladies I Have Loved and Lost"

George Washington University conferred upon me the degree of Doctor of Letters in 1921.* Its president, Dr. William Miller Collier, thus addressed me as he handed me the scroll:

"Julia Marlowe Sothern, foremost living actress in tragic and romantic roles, greatest interpreter of the Immortal Bard of Avon. You have made letters to live in the hearts of myriads and have so instructed and inspired them that all who have seen and heard you with universal admiration and gratitude exclaim in the couplet of Thomas Heywood:

" 'The world's a theatre, the earth's a stage
Which God and Nature do with actors fill.' "

In comment on the occasion the Philadelphia *Evening Bulletin* published this editorial.

DOCTOR JULIA MARLOWE

A graceful compliment was paid to the women of the stage when Julia Marlowe was included in the list of distinguished persons to receive honorary degrees at the centenary of George Washington University. This delightful actress is

* Julia Marlowe was the first actress in America to receive this degree from an American university. Mr. Sothern, who had previously been awarded the same distinction by the same institution, had been the first American actor so honored. A second doctorate would be given Miss Marlowe by Columbia University.

218

now a Doctor of Letters, the first player of her sex to receive similar academic honors in America.

During a career extending beyond thirty years, Miss Marlowe has been identified with the drama that uplifts the cultural standards of audiences. She has brought mental qualities of a high order and exceptional artistic gifts to the interpretation and personification of Shakespeare's heroines.

If at times, Miss Marlowe has lent her fine histrionic endowments and her arch vivacity to plays that fell below her artistic stature, such roles as she had in "When Knighthood Was in Flower" and other "romantic" specimens were relatively sparse. None of the famous actresses of the past, back to and including Sarah Siddons, appeared in so few inferior plays as Miss Marlowe.

Alas, poor *Knighthood!* I cannot treat it with ingratitude. I owe much to that play and much to the people who found entertainment and pleasure in its story. Along with other plays, it was a ladder for my young ambition. I cannot turn my back on them nor scorn them.

During our tour of 1919–20, Mr. Sothern's brother died in Los Angeles. Sam Sothern had come to America with Edward when he returned from his second trip in the cause of the Y.M.C.A. The former's health, never very robust, had declined during the war when, though acting in Sir James Barrie's *Dear Brutus* in London, he undertook the job of receiving and training horses for the forces in France. After a night performance he would go down to Tilbury Docks and in the cold, raw dawn await the arrival of the consignment of horses, ride with them through the city to their destination and later spend strenuous days in breaking in untrained animals. Sam had always been a rider from childhood and ever a devoted hunting man. That was all he had to offer to the England he loved, and he gave it. Twice he had tried to join the armed forces but had been refused. As surely as any man he gave his life for his country.

The American climate helped him for a time, but in New York he insisted on accepting a four weeks' engagement in the American production of *Dear Brutus*. Then he went to Los Angeles where he played in moving pictures. He grew weaker, and my husband, alarmed by his letters, sent Frank Colfax to Los Angeles to bring him to us in New York. He died before the arrival of Frank, who wired us the sad news.

My husband was on the stage going through the difficult scene in *Twelfth Night* where Malvolio is the prey of the conspirators and receives the tricksters' letter. It was his custom to rehearse this complicated scene carefully while the stage was being set. As he stood there superintending the setting and thinking over his lines, his dresser handed him a telegram. Edward read it, then as the curtain rose, he went onstage and played out the scene.

Two more close to us died that year: Frank Colfax, for thirty-five years my devoted friend and servant as he elected to be, and Rowland Buckstone, Mr. Sothern's inseparable comrade since infancy. For twenty years the latter had been a tower of strength in our productions.

They and many others, now gone, had given us of their talent and their strength. I shall recall always the laughter and with sadness the parties we gave every Christmas on the stage of any theatre in which we happened to be playing. At those festivities the whole company—actors, stagehands, wardrobe people, dressers, managers—were gathered together after the play. Great tables were stretched along the footlights and up each side of the stage, and at the back was erected a platform on which a sort of variety show was given. The entertainment was a "take-off" on all the happenings of the season. No strangers were ever admitted, first of all because they might have placed some restraint upon the proceedings, and secondly because the many allusions to the events of the year and the personal references would have been Greek to them. A great Christmas tree always stood on one side and on it were our gifts. Buckstone was always "Father Christmas," with a great fund of quaint observation on all subjects. The programme was usually kept strictly secret from Mr. Sothern and from me, for often we were mercilessly burlesqued in the made entertainment. Now and then Mr. Sothern would be invited to take part, as once when he was the "middle man" in a black-faced minstrel show. He was padded so that he appeared to weigh about four hundred pounds; make-up had given him one of those great mouths which middle men favor, and he wore a shirt stud which had a small electric light in it to be flashed whenever he made a joke. I did not know he was to undertake the new role, so until he spoke his Mr. Bones and Mr. Tambourine talk, I had no idea it was he, and when from that cork-blacked face came my Romeo's voice, I very nearly expired from sheer delight.

Usually our revels concluded with the exchange of presents and then the floor was cleared for dancing. On these occasions one might be sure to discover one's own eccentricities and weak points, for these found their way of necessity into the complicated entertainment. But they were great nights, to be remembered for kindliness. Buckstone was always both a

great "butt" and a great source of entertainment for his innumerable impersonations and was as excited about his presents as a child.

During later years I decided to rest and enjoy a thorough
holiday every other season, so we did not act in 1920–21. We
played our repertoire successfully next season, spent the summer in Switzerland and then took another long year's rest in
1922–23. For the following year we prepared a production of
Cymbeline. The character of Imogen has been a favorite with
all actresses, and the structural shortcomings of the play have
been forgiven on account of the heroine's exquisite protrayal.
I had played Imogen in my earlier years and wanted to have
that satisfaction once more. Mr. Sothern and I prepared a
beautiful production of the play and spent a fortune on the
equipment, I must say for our own satisfaction as much as for
that of the public.

The defects of the play as a play are so well known that it
did not occur to us they would at this day stand in the way of
its popular appeal. The convention which permits Rosalind,
when in man's attire, to escape recognition by Orlando, and
Portia, when robed as the Doctor of Law, to be unknown to
Bassanio, which also so effectually disguises Viola—that convention, we believed, would still prevail in favor of Imogen.
But alas, we counted without the host of new movements which
call a spade a spade and will on no account be persuaded for
the sake of a fairy tale to accept it as a silver spoon, or a magic
wand, or any such foolishness. *Cymbeline* was no fable for the
adult theatre which had recently discovered that *As You Like It*

was a bad play even when produced by a popular actress. There promise to be hard times for those who believe in fairies.

The fabric of Shakespeare's fancy was picked to pieces as though it had been one of the structures of Mr. Ibsen. It is true that *Cymbeline* has at no time been one of Shakespeare's most popular plays, and it is certainly somewhat diffuse in its action. Still it has appealed to many men and women on account of its poetry and the exquisite character of its heroine. It is the play which Tennyson held in his hand when he died. "Give me my Shakespeare," said the failing poet and opened the book. With his finger on the line, "Hang there like fruit, my soul, till the tree die," he crossed the bar. But, of course, Tennyson was of the Victorian Age.

What have been the satisfactions of my life in the theatre? I suppose I had—at least I have been accredited with it—a natural flair for acting. This is inborn, no doubt, as is that for painting or music; one hears of prodigies in those arts. Every child is a born actor, a born pretender. "Let's pretend," is one of his earliest cries. Life is so sad, so monotonous for most people that they are only saved from seeking death by the relief of the fancy. We all are aware of that, and the little child seeks Fairyland. I sought it and I found it in the theatre. This is the land of dreams. This is the harbor of content. Here we may anchor far from the weary world and in our glowing thought be kings and queens. We may be lovers no matter how unlovely, we may be sought, no matter how unlikely to be loved. Such is the origin of all creeds. A longing for perfect good is the flower of imagination which we call "God"—something happier, nobler, more fortunate and wiser than ourselves, possessing courage, beauty, power greater than our own, and able to confer immortal bliss as we can variously comprehend it.

The attraction of the play is to "show us to ourselves as we might be. . . ." But when that ingenuous desire for content passes, and we want to see ourselves mirrored in the pictures of vice and excess, the office of the theatre and its value to the city and the state dies. It becomes a menace and no more a solace.

I felt that as a child and even more as I grew older. As I found refuge from the burden of existence, I wanted to lift it for others. "The Land of Romance"—for that I was bound, and I desired those who were tired or troubled to follow me. The greatest satisfaction I have, now that life is looking toward the west is that I believe I did give gladness. I have known so many poor girls who have seized my hand outside the stage door and thanked me for the glimpses of hope and joy and love they would never have known but for the play.

How can sordid plays give such women comfort? You may say they are deluded by false pictures of happiness which does not exist. Then are we deluded by Heaven and by God; and if I am to be deluded, let it be by the persuasion that all will be fair and just rather than by the conviction that all will be base and pitiless. And let me die happy in my belief in what is not, rather than in terror and despair of that which is. I hate "slices of life" which make one loathe existence and despise mankind. Why should we invite monstrous creatures, abhorrent and obscene, to intrude into our pleasant land of *make-believe*? They are the fancies which terrify and undo the poor wretches who now and then proclaim the end of the world and who are unaware that the world begins anew each day. The poet's word, "Every moment dies a man, every moment one is born," can be interpreted to signify that for each one of us the Old Self is each instant cast away and may be cleansed and renewed within the hour. This is the appeal of the play. "*My* courage, *my* love, *my* sacrifice is there. Thus and so do *I* believe, thus suffer, thus forgive, and if need be thus nobly die." But if the sordid story says, "Thus I wallow," and "Thus debauch my soul," that's quite another matter.

I have delighted all my life in the theatre. I have been happy and proud in the conviction that I was contributing to the heart's ease of great numbers of people. That I loved the work and profited at last—that, too, was part of my happiness, and as I close the stage door for the last time, it is with a sigh that not again shall I feel the thrill which lifted up my heart when I played the great roles born of the greatest intellect of all the ages. It is with pride in my calling that I think of him as an actor, busy with his craft, loved by his brother actors—the gentle Shakespeare, eager to be respected, to be known as a gentleman of good report, a soul of infinite pity and one who understood man's strength and weakness with a sweeter charity than any being who has ever lived—save only One.

What, then, is the moral I can offer from my experience as an actress? How can I aid women who come after me and who may incline toward a stage career? I have tried to show the qualities of endurance and purpose which are indispensable to the sort of struggle upon which I entered. Each one must be the judge of herself. There are lesser prizes than that to which I aspired; a woman may make a living and lead a self-respecting life on the stage and may not suffer more hardship than she would in other walks of life. The vagabond days of the theatre are in a great degree past; yet if one is eager to gain experience, one may still find adventure in companies whose fortunes are governed by the wind. As in every other calling, knowledge is power, ability is money. There is no place for the charlatan, the sluggard, the pretender; he may prevail for a moment, but shortly he is discarded.

To those who accept the long apprenticeship of the law, of medicine, of Holy Orders, and to those who enter the various trades where skill is essential before one can achieve any remuneration at all—bricklaying, for example—the situation of the would-be actor is irritating. Such may perhaps reason: here is a man who simply because he is alive, with no knowledge whatever of his craft is provided with an instructor in the shape of a stage manager, provided with costumes and every accessory, and given a salary which, according to agreement, must not be less than thirty dollars a week in New York and thirty-five dollars a week on tour. Such an entirely uninformed and entirely unaccomplished man, frequently without education and generally without any special knowledge, is permitted to make a weekly wage which would be comforting to bank clerks whose integrity and ability has been submitted to the most desperate investigation. It is true that the enterprise to which he is attached may disintegrate at any moment and is not founded on rock as is the bank, but it is also true that he himself is an element of uncertainty. Yet he and his kind are essential and cannot be dispensed with. One must have crowds. There must be soldiers, courtiers, onlookers, participants of all sorts; and these must live, they must be maintained in health if only that time spent in training them shall not be wasted in training others. Therefore they must be well fed and clothed. Mark Antony must address a Roman mob. There must be rival forces of Capulets and Montagues.

It is true that I myself rose from such humble beginning, and my husband also came from the ranks. A novice, man or woman, would be unwise to scorn first steps. What I have endeavored to point out is the labor which is involved in the greater prize. Nothing less than sincere love for the actor's life can make such slavery as mine endurable. As Ruskin states it:

> I say first—love for the art which you practise. Be assured that if any other motive becomes a leading one in your mind as the principal one for exertion except your love of art—that moment it is all over with your art. If it come to a fair question whether you are to please the Mob—or do the thing as you know it ought to be done—(and you can't do both)— and choose to please the Mob—it's all over with you. There's no hope for you—nothing that you can do will ever be worth a man's glance as he passes by.

It is not, however, in so solemn, nor with so stern an admonition that I would end my contact with the patient reader who may have accompanied me so far upon this voyage of remembrance, should he or she, moved, perhaps, by kindly recollection, wonder if the player of so many parts sits solitary amid the relics of the past. Let it be said that I rejoice still in the company of those fair women whom it has been my privilege to impersonate. I am glad that I was not compelled to become superfluous on the stage. While I am well aware that when the play is over, "the best in this kind are but shadows," I look back on the conflict with a heart which sometimes quickens, even at those moments of defeat which taught me to achieve my modest victory.

After some few years of illness due to the strain of laborious days, I am once more strong and well and willing enough, apart from the pay, to watch the world go by. To those who, for love or money, would lure me back to the theatre, I mention a picture in *Punch* by George Du Maurier wherein a little girl is going upstairs. Her small brother calls to her, "Ethel! I want you." And she replies, "Thank you, Eric, but I want myself."

As I have said, I am happy in remembering the parts I have played—those dear, cherished ladies of Shakespeare's. Let my curtain speech here be the ballade written by my husband for me to recite at a banquet in my honor when I retired.

"MY COACH! GOOD NIGHT, SWEET LADIES!"

> I, dreaming, walked in Arden's wood,
>   Where, Dream of Dreams, roamed Rosaline.
> Demure Viola thoughtful stood
>   Beneath the scented Eglantine.
> Lo! Saucy Beatrice! who, long syne,
>   Hath learned of scornful pride the cost.
> Her eyes from leafy ambush shine—
>   Sweet ladies, I have loved and lost!
>
> The Fair Ophelia, from the flood,
>   Waves a pale hand in parting sign.
> Flaunts Kate the Curst—in Rebel mood;
>   Weeps Cawdor's Queen incarnadine.

Sad Juliet sighs. Her love divine
   By cruel stars forever cross'd.
Here Imogen flees Cymbeline,
   Sweet ladies, I have loved and lost!

Portia who, from the bond of blood,
   Diverted Shylock's fierce design.
Great Egypt's Queen, whom Caesar woo'd,
   Strays here from fields of Proserpine.
Deep drank I of your wisdom's wine,
   Quaffed I your wit, ye radiant host.
Farewell! Your service I resign;
   Sweet ladies, I have loved and lost!

Your hands! Your lips! Yea, thine and thine,
   Hearts debonair—Souls tempest-toss'd—
Your constant Shrine, this heart of mine,
   Sweet ladies, I have loved and lost!

chapter 20 *

Golden Voice

Julia Marlowe and E. H. Sothern took their last bow as stars together and retired in 1924. The play was over, the curtain down. The players stepped back out of the blaze of footlights into the shadows. As Miss Marlowe told her husband-biographer, she was glad she need not linger too long on the boards, an aging actress seeking to revive past glories. She had stood not on the order of her going but made a timely exit.

It had been a wise though not an easy decision, for she still possessed her full powers. A matured art had sustained the "virginal innocence and youthful fire" of her early Juliet. As late as 1921 when she played the part, a New York *Times* critic had written, "It was difficult to realize that the years had rolled by. There was the self-same musical voice, the identical triumphant delivery, the unchanged girlishness that Julia Marlowe brought to us when she first appeared."

Her remarkable career in the theatre—it was forty-six years since her debut at the age of thirteen in the children's company of *H.M.S. Pinafore*—had won her rich rewards, fully earned, amply deserved. The fact that laurels in profusion and wealth had crowned her Shakespearean repertoire, played with her husband, was her special joy.

* Since E. H. Sothern's story of Julia Marlowe ends with their retirement as co-stars (subsequently he made a number of appearances singly), the editor has written this final chapter to cover the intervening years to Miss Marlowe's death in 1950. It is based on information furnished by some of her long-time friends and on material from research sources.

After their retirement the Sotherns traveled widely as they always had, but now the grueling theatrical tours that had taxed their strength lay behind them, and their journeys, for pleasure and rest, took them abroad for long sojourns. They lived quietly in Switzerland and the Riviera, Paris and Florence, and spent winters in Cairo under the warm Egyptian sun and many springs in the England they both loved. That was the country of her birth and his upbringing, the scene of some of their most cherished triumphs. Doubtless Arthur Symons's high praise of the performances often came to their minds: "We have actresses who have many kinds of charm, actors who have many kinds of useful talent; but have we in our whole island two actors capable of giving so serious, so intelligent, so carefully finished, so vital an interpretation of Shakespeare, or, indeed, of rendering any form of poetic drama on the stage as the Englishman and Englishwoman who came to us . . . in the guise of Americans: Julia Marlowe and Edward Sothern?" For the Sotherns, Shakespeare's eulogy, "This blessed plot, this earth, this realm, this England," spoke eloquently. Despite their ties with America, the land of their adoption, they arranged that London's Brompton Cemetery be their last resting place.

During residences abroad theirs was often the company of old friends, seldom stage people: Robert H. Davis (Bob Davis, the New York *Sun* columnist and magazine editor) and his wife; Robert Hichens, the British author who wrote *The Garden of Allah* and many other novels. Mary Daly, "Teresa" of long and faithful service, continued in attendance until age and illness compelled her retirement.

Affectionately these friends of years called Mrs. Sothern

"Lady Julia" and found undiminished in her the charm, the gracious dignity and warmhearted appeal countless audiences had known. Her lovely speaking voice was as golden as ever.* Wherever she was, her birthday was remembered with flowers from her many admirers. Edward Sothern, occupying himself with writing and painting, remained handsome and debonair, still the romantic hero who had gained such acclaim in *If I Were King* and as Romeo.

"The plays are always there," Edward Sothern once had said, "but to play them best your heart must be seized upon." That was as true of the marriage of these two who had starred as Sothern and Marlowe—their companionship remained the happy one it was because their hearts had been seized upon, and since they had no children, their lives were wrapped up in each other. Readers of the foregoing chapters of this book, a husband's fond and proud record of his wife's achievement, cannot doubt their devotion.

They were parted in 1933 when Mr. Sothern died at the age of seventy-four. Sorely missing "dear Edward," as she always spoke of him, Julia Marlowe, accompanied by a maid, continued to spend much time abroad until war clouds, which had driven her from England in 1914, gathered again. Before hurrying home from Switzerland in 1939, she wrote Mrs. Davis a prophetic letter with a keen analysis of Hitler's character. "We are dealing with an abnormal man, who is constantly manifesting a deep depression at recurring intervals, or mad rages on the least provocation—when he is thwarted in any way," she

---

* In 1929 Miss Marlowe received a gold medal award from the American Academy of Arts and Letters "for clarity and melody in the use of the English language."

observed. "If he finds everything going against him and his hopes are gone, he may as a final gesture bombard London and Paris ere he leaves this terrestrial globe. But he will try to make a highly dramatic gesture, poor wretch!"

Back in the United States, Julia Marlowe settled at the Hotel Plaza, New York City, in a comfortable apartment decorated with portraits of Edward Sothern as Hamlet and herself as Ophelia, along with many other mementos. However, she no longer liked to be recognized in public and refused to attend the theatre, even Shakespearean plays. She rejected radio offers although that medium would have been an ideal one for such a voice as hers. While her retirement was complete, she was by no means a recluse, and she did not deny those who sought to honor her. In 1943, Columbia University conferred on her a second doctorate of letters, its citation given by President Nicholas Murray Butler:

> "Born in England and receiving in the United States her education and training in the dramatic art; steadily gaining through a long period of years increasing reputation and charm upon the stage as she fascinated one great audience after another; as has been well said of her 'she made Love and Hope blend'; and holds a place of outstanding excellence in the history of the modern theater."

That same year Julia Marlowe made another of her rare public appearances when at the Museum of the City of New York she opened an exhibit of costumes and other tokens of her stage career she had presented. Her gift was largely inspired by her affectionate remembrance of William Seymour, her stage director for years, and her friendship for his daughter, May

Davenport Seymour, curator of the museum's theatre collection. On display were costumes and wigs Miss Marlowe had worn as Juliet, Viola, Katharine, Portia, Lady Teazel and others, along with costume designs, prompt books, letters, scrapbooks and hundreds of photographs. As she stood before a background of the gowns of Shakespearean heroines she had played so beautifully, she recited the graceful ballade Mr. Sothern had written to her, "Fair Ladies I Have Loved and Lost."

She still loved the daily walks in Central Park she first had taken as a young girl, when she came to New York determined to be a great actress and practiced her parts and mirthful laughter as she strolled. Always her goal was Shakespeare's statue at the southern end of the Mall. How often through the years had she made those pilgrimages, especially on the Bard's birthday. She must have remembered with a smile the ceremony at which Edward Sothern had made a speech, and a twittering dowager had seized his hand and exclaimed, "Oh, that was lovely! I'm so glad I managed to get here. Oh, thank you, Sir Marlowe!" "Madam," Edward had suavely replied, "you confer two quite unmerited distinctions upon me—a knighthood and my wife's name."

Julia Marlowe's devotion to Shakespeare burned as ardently as ever, and she frequently read passages to the blind and to her friends in that golden voice of hers. Perhaps she recalled that day in her girlhood when her mother bought an illustrated volume of Shakespeare's plays and a Bible from a book agent, and it was the former for which she longed and pledged her allowance and extra housework. For now she had come to know and love the Scriptures also and those who heard her recite the

Twenty-third Psalm never forgot the fervor and stately cadence with which she spoke it. She gave generously of her time as a worker for St. James Protestant Episcopal Church. Once at a parish dinner she recited Julia Ward Howe's *Battle Hymn of the Republic*, and the magic of her speech thrilled every listener.

Mrs. Sothern, making a will, left sums to St. James Church and to the Cathedral of St. John the Divine in Edward's memory and her own and again to his in a bequest to his beloved club, The Players. Two nieces, her only surviving relatives, were remembered. A legacy left her by Mary Daly, "my devoted friend and companion," was passed on to St. Patrick's Cathedral. Manuscripts, books and other memorabilia went to the New York Public Library where they augment a rich store of Marlowe material, collected and presented by her admirers.

Among the charitable bequests, a very considerable one to the Community Service Society had an almost casual origin. Howard Lindsay, the playwright and actor, had volunteered to write various stage people, asking support for the society. Among the names he chose, more or less at random, was Miss Marlowe's. Few appeals can have met with a more generous response. Julia Marlowe became a contributor to the society, showing particular interest in its camping and health services for children, and finally named it as her residuary legatee. Her bequest eventually included several thousand articles: works of art, silver, jewelry, furs and clothing.

Her money had come from the public, she told friends in her gentle way, and it was only right and fitting that it go back to them.

During the last two years of her life, Julia Marlowe's strong constitution, which had carried her through such long and arduous endeavor, began to weaken. In a phrase of the Bible she knew so well, she reached a day when "all the daughters of music shall be brought low." At eighty-five years of age, she died November 12, 1950, in the arms of her loyal friend, Mrs. Davis.

One wonders whether St. Peter, whose sense of drama was strong as a mortal, may not grant the souls of good actors and actresses leave of absence to return to earth to read their obituaries. These are their final notices, the last of those reviews they scanned so eagerly in their lifetimes the morning after an opening. Surely Julia Marlowe would have been pleased by the glowing tributes paid her.

Articles, editorials and letters recalled how girls of the 'eighties and 'nineties sent her armfuls of roses and violets and were torn between their admiration for her and near-swooning over the leading man; how many poems she inspired and how "she was herself pure poetry in voice, exquisite diction and personal beauty." They praised her Juliet, her Rosalind and Viola, and the grace and spirit with which she played any and all of Shakespeare's lovely and varied women and spoke for them in the most melodious voice on the American stage. "Her portrayals delighted both the average audience and the Shakespearean scholar," a New York *Herald Tribune* editorial declared, "because she brought into her art the courage, the purpose, and the fidelity which made the poet's heroines veritably live again, whether on a stage of Stratford, London or Manhattan. Julia Marlowe was in the true line of the world's great players. She knew their secret and she fulfilled their task. She will be remembered forever in stage annals. She will be missed by those who long kept step with her in time and affection."

The Lady of the Golden Voice is gone, a New York *Times* editorial said in farewell. A quarter of a century had elapsed since her retirement, and there were some, it granted, who did not know her name. "But she belonged to the immortals and on Sunday, at the age of eighty-five, she joined them."